God's Laws and Business

"Wisdom is the principal thing; therefore get wisdom: and
with all thy getting get understanding"
Proverbs 4:7

Joanne P. Horne

WestBow
PRESS
A DIVISION OF THOMAS NELSON

ISBN: 978-1-4497-4893-7 (sc)
ISBN: 978-1-4497-4894-4 (hc)
ISBN: 978-1-4497-4891-3 (e)

Library of Congress Control Number: 2012907253

WestBow Press books may be ordered through booksellers or by contacting:

WestBow Press
A Division of Thomas Nelson
1663 Liberty Drive
Bloomington, IN 47403
www.westbowpress.com
1-(866) 928-1240

Printed in the United States of America

WestBow Press rev. date: 04/26/12

Wisdom is the principal thing; therefore get wisdom: and with all thy getting get understanding.
Proverbs 4:7

To my children, Sean and Faith. Thank you two for all of your moral support and love. I love you with all my heart.

To my mother, Mary Horne, who has gone on to be with the Lord on February 25, 2011, and who introduced me to the word of God. Through her works, they live on.

To my dearest friend, Sylvia R. Young, whom God has bought back into my life for such a time as this, imparting inspiration, encouragement, and strength. Thanks, Syl.

Change your thoughts and you change your world.
Norman Vincent Peale

Contents

Warning

This book, when adhered to and followed, will cause you to take these principles into other areas of your life. This material will help you build your faith to miraculous heights, encouraging you to stand still and see the salvation of the Lord.

Preface

IN 1990, I HAD BEEN employed 5 years for Digital Equipment Corporation, as a Field Service Engineer. I was responsible for all repairs and full time management of two of their Customer Service Repair Centers, one in Melville and the other in Whitestone, N.Y. We serviced over 350 customers on Long Island and Brooklyn-Queens areas. It was during this time that I considered opening my own computer repair company. Digital Equipment Corp. began to consider downsizing. My job was secure, but the thought of a companies' financial position determining my financial status, outright scared me. The decision was a simple, I resigned from my employer to start a Computer Repair business. Being a Christian, I quickly realized that with the freedom of owning a business came a great responsibility to the Lord, not as an employee who keeps the laws of the employer according to the King James Version of the Bible: "Servants, be obedient to them that are your masters according to the flesh, with fear and trembling, in singleness of your heart, as unto Christ; Not with eyeservice, as menpleasers; but as the servants of Christ, doing the will of God from the heart; With good will doing service, as to the Lord, and not to men: Knowing that whatsoever good thing any man doeth, the same shall he receive of the Lord, whether he be bond or free" (Eph. 6:58), but as an employer, casting an equal degree of accountability on me the employer: "And, ye masters, do the same things unto them, forbearing threatening: knowing that your Master also is in heaven; neither is there respect of persons with him" (Eph. 6:59).

With this, I stepped into my new status, believing I would lean on God and he would teach me his business methods. He certainly did not disappoint. He was faithful in doing just that. His principles and standards were extremely different from what I had witnessed in some of the world's leading corporations. I truly thought I was qualified to successfully run a business and maintain my integrity and ethics in God. God's laws, his standards, were much higher. This new process consisted of him dictating and integrating his own laws into my business through my spiritual consciousness. This amazed me. All the knowledge I thought I contained was of little use to me. It just seemed unproductive. Through this technique, God began to give me understanding of what the prophet Isaiah meant when he prophesied,

> For my thoughts are not your thoughts, neither are your ways my ways, saith the LORD. For as the heavens are higher than the earth, so are my ways higher than your ways, and my thoughts than your thoughts. For as the rain cometh down, and the snow from heaven, and returneth not thither, but watereth the earth, and maketh it bring forth and bud, that it may give seed to the sower, and bread to the eater: So shall my word be that goeth forth out of my mouth: it shall not return unto me void, but it shall accomplish that which I please, and it shall prosper in the thing whereto I sent it (Isa. 55:8–11).

God showed me that this word was for me personally, his child. The most important lesson I learned was that, as a blood-bought child of God, I was to please him and he took good pleasure in providing and imparting all his many blessings to me and my household. The Lord taught me to conduct a vibrant, thriving, flourishing business.

God has revealed his methods concerning economics, finance, customer relations, suitable cohesive partnerships, and profitable investments to me over the years. All of his ways are endorsed through the Bible (his holy word or book of instruction) used for the government of our lives.

I wrote this book for the new business owner who seeks insight into the mind of God as it relates to his or her business practices. When you allow God to reign in your life as well as your business, you will have great success in all areas of your existence. After applying these principles, you will trust God and take him at his word. This book challenges Christians to put their faith where they profess it to be, in Our Lord and Savior Jesus Christ.

Otherwise, when he has laid a foundation and is not able to finish,
all who observe it begin to ridicule him.
Luke 14:29

Chapter 1
Weigh the Cost

IN JUNE 1991, I WENT into business for myself. It was the first business I had ever owned. I considered what I was doing in someone else's business and concluded I could do it for myself. Excited and full of faith, I forged ahead. It wasn't long before I realized that, with the freedom to project my own income, which made all possibilities limitless, came accountability to the Lord. Little did I know what Christ meant when he stated, "For unto whomsoever much is given, of him shall be much required: and to whom men have committed much, of him they will ask the more" (Luke 12:48). I was about to experience this saying prove itself to be true indeed, as is everything else that our Lord quoted. The responsibility of being an honest, financially responsible merchant walked hand in hand with being a godly and upright boss.

I had not previously considered the many hats a small business owner is required to wear, including the significantly noble one that bears the label *Christian* on it. Your business ethics and practices will hold a huge pulpit microphone, daily announcing your message to the world. Everyone you partner with in business, employ, layoff, support financially (Community and non-profit organizations) consider your faith. They will either admire your walk with God and inquire about him and his power, or they will curse God because of you. Paul says it right:

> But if you bear the name "Jew" and rely upon the Law and boast in God, and know [His] will and approve the things

that are essential, being instructed out of the Law, and
are confident that you yourself are a guide to the blind,
a light to those who are in darkness, a corrector of the
foolish, a teacher of the immature, having in the Law the
embodiment of knowledge and of the truth, you, therefore,
who teach another, do you not teach yourself? You who
preach that one shall not steal, do you steal? You who
say that one should not commit adultery, do you commit
adultery? You who abhor idols, do you rob temples? You
who boast in the Law, through your breaking the Law, do
you dishonor God? For "the name of God is blasphemed
among the Gentiles because of you," just as it is written.
For indeed circumcision is of value if you practice the Law;
but if you are a transgressor of the Law, your circumcision
has become uncircumcision. So if the uncircumcised
man keeps the requirements of the Law, will not his
uncircumcision be regarded as circumcision? And he who
is physically uncircumcised, if he keeps the Law, will he
not judge you who though having the letter [of the Law]
and circumcision are a transgressor of the Law? For he is
not a Jew who is one outwardly, nor is circumcision that
which is outward in the flesh. But he is a Jew who is one
inwardly; and circumcision is that which is of the heart,
by the Spirit, not by the letter; and his praise is not from
men, but from God (Rom. 2:17–29).

We as blood-bought Christians have a full obligation to live
the gospel we preach. Our behavior has to line up with whom we
profess to be. Our faith must be seen in our works. We believe;
thus, our works reveal what we believe. Paul has challenged us to
practice what we preach.

James also presents his argument to combine our faith
with works, proving the fact that we have faith by our works or
vice versa. He establishes his position on the matter with a few
examples:

What doth it profit, my brethren, if a man say he hath faith, but have not works? can that faith save him? If a brother or sister be naked and in lack of daily food, and one of you say unto them, Go in peace, be ye warmed and filled; and yet ye give them not the things needful to the body; what doth it profit? Even so faith, if it have not works, is dead in itself. Yea, a man will say, Thou hast faith, and I have works: show me thy faith apart from [thy] works, and I by my works will show thee [my] faith. Thou believest that God is one; thou doest well: the demons also believe, and shudder. But wilt thou know, O vain man, that faith apart from works is barren? Was not Abraham our father justified by works, in that he offered up Isaac his son upon the altar? Thou seest that faith wrought with his works, and by works was faith made perfect; and the scripture was fulfilled which saith, And Abraham believed God, and it was reckoned unto him for righteousness; and he was called the friend of God. Ye see that by works a man is justified, and not only by faith. And in like manner was not also Rahab the harlot justified by works, in that she received the messengers, and sent them out another way? For as the body apart from the spirit is dead, even so faith apart from works is dead (Jas. 2:14–26).

James makes a great point. Faith has to be accompanied by action (works) as evidence of things you believe. We must produce the fruit of Christianity if we say we are Christians. This evidence of belief is our works. The works of a man will disclose who he is, good or evil.

When you become a business owner in your community, you suddenly become a local public figure. Business ownership holds within it the potential of aspiring to national public figure status. You could become a very wealthy public figure. Your character will be weighed and laid out for the entire world to see. Your godly reverence will be undeniable evident; equally evident will be your disregard for God. This newfound popularity is a two-edged sword. The blade on the one side can slay the very name of Jesus Christ, or it can be used to perform surgery on the hearts of men, wooing them ever so gently to want to consider Christ. Consciences are pierced through the witnessing of Christian character.

Many benefits are granted to you in business. There will be many temptations and opportunities for gain presented. Your challenge will be to keep in mind that our obligation is to God above everything. Luke tells the story of the various types of temptation that Satan presents to Jesus as a forewarning for us:

> Then Jesus, being filled with the Holy Spirit, returned from the Jordan and was led by the Spirit into the wilderness, being tempted for forty days by the devil. And in those days He ate nothing, and afterward, when they had ended, He was hungry. And the devil said to Him, "If You are the Son of God, command this stone to become bread." But Jesus answered him, saying, "It is written, 'Man shall not live by bread alone, but by every word of God.'" Then the devil, taking Him up on a high mountain, showed Him all the kingdoms of the world in a moment of time. And the devil said to Him, "All this authority I will give You, and their glory; for this has been delivered to me, and I give it to whomever I wish. Therefore, if You will worship before me, all will be Yours." And Jesus answered and said to him, "Get behind Me, Satan! For it is written, 'You shall worship the Lord your God, and Him only you shall serve.'" Then he brought him to Jerusalem, set him on the pinnacle of the temple, and said to Him, "If You are the Son of God, throw Yourself down from here. For it is written: 'He shall give His angels charge over you, To keep you,' and, 'In their hands they shall bear you up, Lest you dash your foot against a stone.'" And Jesus answered and said to him, "It has been said, 'You shall not tempt the

Lord your God.'" Now when the devil had ended every temptation, he departed from Him until an opportune time (Luke 4:1–13).

Here Luke laid out an example of how we are to respond during temptation. Stand sure on the written word of God. Temptation will present itself in various forms.

There are Christian business owners who honor God in their establishments, but there are more who don't. They make tons of excuses as to why they reacted in a certain manner in response to specific issues. It really boils down to a lack of faith in God and his word concerning the issues they face. But be assured that suffering likewise accompanies the God-fearing businessman who lives by the every word that proceeded from the mouth of God. Doing business with today's consumers while adhering to the word of God will be sure to try your faith. Your relationship with God will either grow or begin to fade away. Some Christians will grow in grace, and others will fall away from the faith. Jesus explained how this works:

> The same day went Jesus out of the house, and sat by the sea side. And great multitudes were gathered together unto him, so that he went into a ship, and sat; and the whole multitude stood on the shore. And he spake many things unto them in parables, saying, Behold, a sower went forth to sow; And when he sowed, some seeds fell by the way side, and the fowls came and devoured them up: Some fell upon stony places, where they had not much earth: and forthwith they sprung up, because they had no deepness of earth: And when the sun was up, they were scorched; and because they had no root, they withered away. And some fell among thorns; and the thorns sprung up, and choked them: But other fell into good ground, and brought forth fruit, some an hundredfold, some sixtyfold, some thirtyfold. Who hath ears to hear, let him hear.

And the disciples came, and said unto him, Why speakest thou unto them in parables? He answered and said unto them, because it is given unto you to know the mysteries of the kingdom of heaven, but to them it is not given. For whosoever hath, to him shall be given, and he shall have more abundance (Matt. 13:1–12).

You fall away because you don't possess the seed. He warns that, if for any reason you are unable to receive, hold onto, or nurture the seed (word of God) that is sown by the sower, it will fade away. For those who do have the seed, the seed will multiply , some one hundred times, some sixty, and some thirty. You will grow victoriously withstanding the trials. Through the trials, you flourish. If you have the seed, he will grow it. The majority of our spiritual growth will be accomplished within our trials.

It is important for us to count the cost before starting your own business and hanging your "I am a Christian business" sign out front. Jesus gives us wisdom:

For which of you, intending to build a tower, does not sit down first and count the cost, whether he has enough to finish it. lest, after he has laid the foundation, and is not able to finish, all who see it begin to mock him, saying, "This man began to build and was not able to finish." Or what king, going to make war against another king, does not sit down first and consider whether he is able with ten thousand to meet him who comes against him with twenty thousand? Or else, while the other is still a great way off, he sends a delegation and asks conditions of peace. So likewise, whoever of you does not forsake all that he has cannot be my disciple. Salt is good; but if the salt has lost its flavor, how shall it be seasoned? It is neither fit for the land nor for the dunghill, but men throw it out. He who has ears to hear, let him hear (Luke 14:28–35)!

Do a business analysis, and draw up a business plan. We tend to rely totally on God to do what we should do for ourselves. God cannot be held responsible for not giving you a heads-up on the number of other businesses like yours selling the exact same products or services in the area or how many people will frequent your establishment for that matter. He gives us a sound mind to do these things for ourselves. Some of us are so "heavenly minded we are no earthly good" to our own selves or anybody else. You will need to be diligent and in the moment for this one. Count the cost before you begin the task to determine if you have enough to finish.

Bear this in mind. You are not only called to invest in the principles and ethics of Our Lord and Savior Jesus Christ. You are also investing in your business. Your name is on the business, and his name is on you.

Be diligent to present yourself approved to God as a workman who does not need to be ashamed, accurately handling the word of truth.
2 Timothy 2:15

Chapter 2

Expounding on God's Laws

WITHIN THE HOLY SCRIPTURES, THE books of Leviticus, Exodus, and Deuteronomy contain the laws of God for the government of God's chosen people. In this chapter, I will discuss the laws of God, which God wrote and gave to Moses for his people to construct a government, which was designed to express the righteous will of God, and to govern their social and religious lives, God complied a written standard he wanted his people to live by. He differentiated his people from other people in the world and gave them their own identity as his people and only his. These laws are coupled with the laws that are written in the mind and on the heart of man, as Jeremiah promised in the scriptures to further identify them. They establish and validate the importance of the birth and death of Jesus Christ, which ushered the presence of the Holy Spirit into the world. Jeremiah prophesied:

> But this is the covenant that I will make with the house of Israel after those days, says the Lord: I will put My law in their minds, and write it on their hearts; and I will be their God, and they shall be My people. No more shall every man teach his neighbor, and every man his brother, saying, "Know the Lord," for they all shall know Me, from the least of them to the greatest of them, says the Lord. For I will forgive their iniquity, and their sin I will remember no more (Jer. 31:27–34).

The books of the law (the Torah, Pentateuch, or first five books of the Bible) were written to aid in governing the Israelites upon their departure from the land of Egypt. The Torah has been useful and is a guide for men to follow, preventing them from violating the rights of other human beings and other life. Most of the laws in the Bible were used as a foundation for laws that the American legislative body implemented. These laws are found in Exodus. The Israelites was given the law to assist them with their individual, moral, and corporate government. These laws helped them understand God's own standards and what he expected of them. They set civil standards for the entire body of Israelites as a nation, rising the living standards within their families and nation as a whole. Some examples of the Law of Moses that have been written and adopted by the American law today are the following:

- "And the man that committed adultery with another man's wife, even he that committeth adultery with his neighbour's wife, the adulterer and the adulteress shall surely be put to death" (Lev. 20:10). In the state of New York, adultery, if proven, is grounds for divorce.
- "And the man that lieth with his father's wife hath uncovered his father's nakedness: both of them shall surely be put to death; their blood shall be upon them" (Lev. 20:11). This would be incest.
- "If a man also lie with mankind, as he lieth with a woman, both of them have committed an abomination: they shall surely be put to death; their blood shall be upon them" (Lev. 20:13). This would fall under sodomy.
- "And if a man take a wife and her mother, it is wickedness: they shall be burnt with fire, both he and they; that there be no wickedness among you"

(Lev. 20:14). This would be polygamy and incest in the United States.

* "And if a man lie with a beast, he shall surely be put to death: and ye shall slay the beast" (Lev. 20:15). This is bestiality in the United States.

Then there's the Ten Commandments:

And God spake all these words, saying, I am the LORD thy God, which have brought thee out of the land of Egypt, out of the house of bondage. Thou shalt have no other gods before me. Thou shalt not make unto thee any graven image, or any likeness of any thing that is in heaven above, or that is in the earth beneath, or that is in the water under the earth. Thou shalt not bow down thyself to them, nor serve them: for I the LORD thy God am a jealous God, visiting the iniquity of the fathers upon the children unto the third and fourth generation of them that hate me; And shewing mercy unto thousands of them that love me, and keep my commandments. Thou shalt not take the name of the LORD thy God in vain; for the LORD will not hold him guiltless that taketh his name in vain. Remember the sabbath day, to keep it holy. Six days shalt thou labour, and do all thy work: But the seventh day is the sabbath of the LORD thy God: in it thou shalt not do any work, thou, nor thy son, nor thy daughter, thy manservant, nor thy maidservant, nor thy cattle, nor thy stranger that is within thy gates: For in six days the LORD made heaven and earth, the sea, and all that in them is, and rested the seventh day: wherefore the LORD blessed the sabbath day, and hallowed it (Ex. 20:1–11).

Many different Christian and non-Christian denominations honor this commandment by worshiping on the seventh day, a day of rest.

"Honour thy father and thy mother: that thy days may be long upon the land which the LORD thy God giveth thee. Thou shalt not kill" (Ex. 20:12–13). Murder, as we know, is against the law.

"Thou shalt not commit adultery. Thou shalt not steal. Thou shalt not bear false witness against thy neighbour. Thou shalt not covet thy neighbour's house, thou shalt not covet thy neighbour's wife, nor his manservant, nor his maidservant, nor his ox, nor his ass, nor any thing that is thy neighbour's" (Ex. 20:14–17).

The law given to the people of that era is still essential and necessary today. These laws are designed to protect the righteous from the wicked, so says Paul:

> Let every soul be subject unto the higher powers. For there is no power but of God: the powers that be are ordained of God. Adhere to the magistrates and higher authorities that bear rule over us, for God placed them there. Whosoever therefore resisteth the power, resisteth the ordinance of God: and they that resist shall receive to themselves damnation. For rulers are not a terror to good works, but to the evil. Wilt thou then not be afraid of the power? do that which is good, and thou shalt have praise of the same: For he is the minister of God to thee for good. But if thou do that which is evil, be afraid; for he beareth not the sword in vain: for he is the minister of God, a revenger to execute wrath upon him that doeth evil (Rom. 13:1–4).

He says that, if you do well, he will protect you. But if you are evil, he is there to execute wrath as a minister of God. He goes on to say that we need this authority in the world over us in order to keep us morally sound. "Wherefore ye must needs be subject, not only for wrath, but also for conscience sake. For this cause pay ye tribute also: for they are God's ministers, attending continually upon this very thing" (Rom. 13:5–6).

Finally, he tells us to pay our taxes so they may do their jobs for society.

So where does Christians stand today with the law? Matthew quotes Jesus Christ himself: "Think not that I am come to destroy the law, or the prophets: I am not come to destroy, but to fulfil. For verily I say unto you, Till heaven and earth pass, one jot or one tittle shall in no wise pass from the law, till all be fulfilled. Whosoever therefore shall break one of these least commandments, and shall teach men so, he shall be called the least in the kingdom of heaven: but whosoever shall do and teach them, the same shall be called great in the kingdom of heaven. For I say unto you, That except your righteousness shall exceed the righteousness of the scribes and Pharisees, ye shall in no case enter into the kingdom of heaven" (Matt. 5:17–20).

So what exactly are we reading here? Jesus says we must keep the old law. Then he says, "Ye have heard that it hath been said, An eye for an eye, and a tooth for a tooth: But I say unto you, That ye resist not evil: but whosoever shall smite thee on thy right cheek, turn to him the other also. And if any man will sue thee at the law, and take away thy coat, let him have thy cloke also. And whosoever shall compel thee to go a mile, go with him twain. Give to him that asketh thee, and from him that would borrow of thee turn not thou away" (Matt. 5:38–42).

He asks us to do even more. He asks us to allow ourselves to be giving and forgiving and not retaliate to those who would misuse and abuse us. This form of submission could only be adhered to by the receipt of the Holy Spirit as our comforter. This new criteria for keeping the law, which Christ spoke of, was only possible through the help of the Holy Ghost. Oh, how disillusioned the hearers must have been that heard this speech.

Jesus himself begins to reveal this mystery: "Nevertheless I tell you the truth; It is expedient for you that I go away: for if I go not away, the Comforter will not come unto you; but if I depart, I will send him unto you. And when he is come, he will reprove the world of sin, and of righteousness, and of judgment: Of sin, because they believe not on me; Of righteousness, because I go to my Father, and ye see me no more; Of judgment, because the prince of this world is judged. I have yet many things to say unto you, but ye cannot bear them now. Howbeit when he, the Spirit of truth, is come, he will guide you into all truth: for he shall not speak of himself; but whatsoever he shall hear, that shall he speak: and he will shew you things to come. He shall glorify me: for he shall receive of mine, and shall shew it unto you. All things that the Father hath are mine: therefore said I, that he shall take of mine, and shall shew it unto you" (John 16:7–15).

The Holy Spirit had not been given unto men yet, which was to encourage and teach man from within his own consciences and heart to keep the law. Working from within. Jesus talked of this event: "If ye love me, keep my commandments. And I will pray the Father, and he shall give you another Comforter, that he may abide with you for ever; Even the Spirit of truth; whom the world cannot receive, because it seeth him not, neither knoweth him: but ye know him; for he dwelleth with you, and shall be in you" (John 14:15–17).

And it continues: "These things have I spoken unto you, being yet present with you. But the Comforter, which is the Holy Ghost, whom the Father will send in my name, he shall teach you all things, and bring all things to your remembrance, whatsoever I have said unto you. Peace I leave with you, my peace I give unto you: not as the world giveth, give I unto you. Let not your heart be troubled, neither let it be afraid" (John 14:25–27). He spoke of a Comforter who would dwell in us and teach us all things.

Now, after the death of Christ Jesus, Paul explains to the church in Rome, "Or do you not know, brethren (for I speak to those who know the law), that the law has dominion over a man as long as he lives? For the woman who has a husband is bound by the law to her husband as long as he lives. But if the husband dies, she is released from the law of her husband. So then if, while her husband lives, she marries another man, she will be called an adulteress; but if her husband dies, she is free from that law, so that she is no adulteress, though she has married another man. Therefore, my brethren, you also have become dead to the law through the body of Christ, that you may be married to another—to Him who was raised from the dead, that we should bear fruit to God. For when we were in the flesh, the sinful passions which were aroused by the law were at work in our members to bear fruit to death. But now we have been delivered from the law, having died to what we were held by, so that we should serve in the newness of the Spirit and not in the oldness of the letter" (Rom. 7:1–6).

Paul assures us that we can rest in knowing that we have died to the law because we have the spirit inside of us directing us to keep the law.

The new law could have two effects on the old law:
- The new law can put new life and power in the old law, therefore adding something to it.
- The new law can remove and replace the old law pertaining to it.

Jesus states, "For assuredly, I say to you, till heaven and earth pass away, one jot or one tittle will by no means pass from the law till all is fulfilled" (Matt. 5:18). The whole issue was laid out before us through his statement here. Jesus came to add to the law. The new law gives power and life to the old law. Within the Christian believer, it becomes an inner force shaping the character from within. Under the new law, virtue takes form with the help of the Holy Ghost and becomes a natural force that takes form shaping us from within. This pair, coupled together, secures spiritual inheritance.

Paul says, "For he is our peace, who hath made both one, and hath broken down the middle wall of partition between us; Having abolished in his flesh the enmity, even the law of commandments contained in ordinances; for to make in himself of twain one new man, so making peace; And that he might reconcile both unto God in one body by the cross, having slain the enmity thereby: And came and preached peace to you which were afar off, and to them that were nigh. For through him we both have access by one Spirit unto the Father. Now therefore ye are no more strangers and foreigners, but fellow citizens with the saints, and of the household of God; And are built upon the foundation of the apostles and prophets, Jesus Christ himself being the chief corner stone; In whom all the building fitly framed together groweth unto an holy temple in the Lord: In whom ye also are builded together for an habitation of God through the Spirit" (Eph. 2:14–22). And he also says, "There is therefore now no condemnation to those who are in Christ Jesus, who do not walk according to the flesh, but according to the Spirit" (Rom. 8:1).

We are only able to keep the laws of God by the receiving of the Holy Spirit, which was sent back to us from heaven after Jesus's death. He is our helper. Jesus states before his death, "These things I have spoken to you while being present with you. But the Helper, the Holy Spirit, whom the Father will send in My name, He will teach you all things, and bring to your remembrance all things that I said to you. Peace I leave with you, My peace I give to you; not as the world gives do I give to you. Let not your heart be troubled, neither let it be afraid" (John 14:25–27). The keys to heaven lie in this fact.

Let us walk in faith and integrity knowing that Jesus's life was laid down at the cross at Calvary so we could have this privilege. The author of Hebrews writes, "For if we sin willfully after that we have received the knowledge of the truth, there remaineth no more sacrifice for sins, But a certain fearful looking for of judgment and fiery indignation, which shall devour the adversaries. He that despised Moses' law died without mercy under two or three witnesses: Of how much sorer punishment, suppose ye, shall he be thought worthy, who hath trodden under foot the Son of God, and hath counted the blood of the covenant, wherewith he was sanctified, an unholy thing, and hath done despite unto the Spirit of grace? For we know him that hath said, Vengeance belongeth unto me, I will recompense, saith the Lord. And again, The Lord shall judge his people. It is a fearful thing to fall into the hands of the living God" (Heb. 10:26–31).

So we come to this conclusion on the matter that King Solomon states so eloquently, "Let us hear the conclusion of the whole matter: Fear God, and keep his commandments: for this is the whole duty of man. For God shall bring every work into judgment, with every secret thing, whether it be good, or whether it be evil" (Eccl. 12:13–14).

We have a duty to keep the commandments of God, and it is honorable before God not to offend the king by breaking governmental laws.

Wisdom is the principal thing; therefore get wisdom: and with all thy getting get understanding.
Proverbs 4:7

Chapter 3
The Wisdom of God

WHEN MAKING DECISIONS IN BUSINESS, you will unquestionably need wisdom. Many opportunities for increasing your bottom line will be presented to you, and with these possibilities will come "the best made plans of men and mice." Making sound decisions will hinge on your collection of information. The fields may look great from the reaper's point of view, but they are certainly no substitute for the knowledge that you gather personally about that field. Our advantage is in having direct access to the creator of all things, the boss, God himself. "The LORD by wisdom founded the earth, By understanding He established the heavens" (Ps. 3:19).

When discussing wisdom, allow me to point out that there are two kinds of wisdom: divine wisdom and worldly wisdom.

- Divine wisdom is wisdom that is communicated to us from the mind of God. It is conveyed by his spirit to us, accompanied by the power of God. We also gain this wisdom as a result our seeking God's thoughts regarding our issues. We can receive wisdom by praying, fasting, and studying God's written word. These actions draw us near to him, by which God's thoughts and laws are acknowledged, understood, and conveyed unto us.

- Worldly wisdom is the wisdom of man without Christ. It is fallible and full of imperfections. Men use it to manipulate and control circumstances in the world markets and other men's lives, aimed at tilting the scales of justice, fame, and fortune in their own favor. Worldly wisdom is often the type of wisdom that is used in the marketplace today.

Let's examine the differences. *Webster New World Dictionary* states wisdom is (1) the quality of being wise; good judgment; (2) learning; knowledge. Some dictionaries describe it to be good sense, wise decisions, accumulated learning, opinion widely held, and sayings. Worldly wisdom is knowledge that specialists or so-called experts in a particular field of study gather over time. Advice is gathered from various sources and helps aid in the betterment of mankind. This advice is called wisdom.

The problem with worldly wisdom today is it is often sold to you. Yes, people profit from disclosing information that might help you, which contains elements of self-serving sins that appoint you as prey for a host of other people and industries that also stand to profit from your ignorance. There you have it, worldly wisdom contaminated by worldly men. What does God's word say about worldly wisdom? "Let no man deceive himself. If any man among you seemeth to be wise in this world, let him become a fool, that he may be wise. For the wisdom of this world is foolishness with God. For it is written, He taketh the wise in their own craftiness. And again, The Lord knoweth the thoughts of the wise, that they are vain" (1 Cor. 3:18–20).

This portion of the scripture clearly states that God puts absolutely no credence or value in the wisdom of men. Not only does he place it in the category of foolishness, he also says that the thoughts of the wise are vain. We have absolutely no excuse for pride in ourselves for our own wisdom, wisdom that we glory in apart from God. Paul explains the wisdom of God so eloquently here,

> For it is written, I will destroy the wisdom of the wise, and will bring to nothing the understanding of the prudent. Where is the wise? Where is the scribe? Where is the disputer of this world? hath not God made foolish the wisdom of this world? For after that in the wisdom of God the world by wisdom knew not God, it pleased God by the foolishness of preaching to save them that believe. For the Jews require a sign, and the Greeks seek after wisdom: But we preach Christ crucified, unto the Jews a stumbling block, and unto the Greeks foolishness; But unto them which are called, both Jews and Greeks, Christ the power of God, and the wisdom of God. Because the foolishness of God is wiser than men; and the weakness of God is stronger than men. For ye see your calling, brethren, how that not many wise men after the flesh, not many mighty, not many noble, are called: But God hath chosen the foolish things of the world to confound the wise; and God hath chosen the weak things of the world to confound the things which are mighty; And base things of the world, and things which are despised, hath God chosen, yea, and things which are not, to bring to nought things that are: That no flesh should glory in his presence. But of him are ye in Christ Jesus, who of God is made unto us wisdom, and righteousness, and sanctification, and redemption: That, according as it is written, He that glorieth, let him glory in the Lord (1 Cor. 1:19–31).

The wisdom of God is God's wisdom accompanied by Christ, the power of God. Paul declares that not many wise, noble, or mighty men are called unto God because God wanted to confound them in their own wisdom. Thus, he chose the things that are despised to contain his wisdom so the wise of this world could not glory in themselves but glory in the Lord instead. We have access to a greater wisdom in that it is God's wisdom. The foolishness of God is wiser than men, and the weakness of God is stronger than men, so says Paul. Now that's powerful. In business while in God is a powerful place to be.

What is the wisdom of God? It is a gift from God. "And I, brethren, when I came to you, came not with excellency of speech or of wisdom, declaring unto you the testimony of God. For I determined not to know anything among you, save Jesus Christ, and him crucified. And I was with you in weakness, and in fear, and in much trembling. And my speech and my preaching was not with enticing words of man's wisdom, but in demonstration of the Spirit and of power: That your faith should not stand in the wisdom of men, but in the power of God" (1 Cor. 2:1–5).

Paul makes clear that he purposely came in the power and demonstration of God's spirit so we would not trust the wisdom of men but the power of God. He was sufficiently educated, equipped to present the gospel in excellent speech. He lays aside his oratorical excellence and philosophical skills to reveal a mystery from God, a more excellent way. Paul continues,

> Howbeit we speak wisdom among them that are perfect: yet not the wisdom of this world, nor of the princes of this world, that come to nought: But we speak the wisdom of God in a mystery, even the hidden wisdom, which God ordained before the world unto our glory: Which none of the princes of this world knew: for had they known it, they would not have crucified the Lord of glory. But as it is written, Eye hath not seen, nor ear heard, neither have entered into the heart of man, the things which God hath prepared for them that love him. But God hath revealed them unto us by his Spirit: for the Spirit searcheth all things, yea, the deep things of God. For what man knoweth the things of a man, save the spirit of man which is in him? even so the things of God knoweth

no man, but the Spirit of God. Now we have received, not the spirit of the world, but the spirit which is of God; that we might know the things that are freely given to us of God. Which things also we speak, not in the words which man's wisdom teacheth, but which the Holy Ghost teacheth; comparing spiritual things with spiritual. But the natural man receiveth not the things of the Spirit of God: for they are foolishness unto him: neither can he know them, because they are spiritually discerned. But he that is spiritual judgeth all things, yet he himself is judged of no man. For who hath known the mind of the Lord, that he may instruct him? But we have the mind of Christ (1 Cor. 6–16).

The mind of Christ gives us the knowledge of God. Because we are still in the physical body, we know the mind of man. These two natures give us the complete advantage in this world. Paul says to the believer, "Therefore let no man glory in men. For all things are yours; Whether Paul, or Apollos, or Cephas, or the world, or life, or death, or things present, or things to come; all are yours; And ye are Christ's; and Christ is God's" (1 Cor. 3:21–23). The world is literately under your feet. God will get all the glory. The world doesn't have a chance. He has made it so we win!

Divine wisdom in business is conveyed from God to us when the believer must make various decisions. We walk by faith and not by sight. We have faith in God and his written word. "Consider it all joy, my brethren, when you encounter various trials, knowing that the testing of your faith produces endurance. And let endurance have its perfect result, so that you may be perfect and complete, lacking in nothing. But if any of you lacks wisdom, let him ask of God, who gives to all generously and without reproach, and it will be given to him. But he must ask in faith without any doubting, for the one who doubts is like the surf of the sea, driven and tossed by the wind. For that man ought not to expect that he will receive anything from the Lord, being a double-minded man, unstable in all his ways" (Jas. 1:2–8).

According to the American Standard Bible, James advises us that we should have joy in the various trials that we are going to face and know that numerous trials will test our faith, producing endurance and the ability to bear prolonged hardships. He says, if we consider it all joy and allow ourselves to go through the complete process, not terminating it in its course, it will work in us a perfect result. We will then lack nothing. James then suggests we ask God for wisdom if we feel we need it, but only in faith, believing he will give it to us. James then cautions us regarding our posture when we ask. It must be anchored and grounded in faith, not doubting.

Job champions for the wisdom of God:

> The tabernacles of robbers prosper, and they that provoke God are secure; into whose hand God bringeth abundantly. But ask now the beasts, and they shall teach thee; and the fowls of the air, and they shall tell thee: Or speak to the earth, and it shall teach thee: and the fishes of the sea shall declare unto thee. Who knoweth not in all these that the hand of the LORD hath wrought this? In whose hand is the soul of every living thing, and the breath of all mankind. Doth not the ear try words? and the mouth taste his meat? With the ancient is wisdom; and in length of days understanding. With him is wisdom and strength, he hath counsel and understanding. Behold, he breaketh down, and it cannot be built again: he shutteth up a man, and there can be no opening. Behold, he withholdeth the waters, and they dry up: also he sendeth them out, and they overturn the earth. With him is strength and wisdom: the deceived and the deceiver are his. He leadeth counsellors away spoiled, and maketh the judges fools. He looseth the bond of kings, and girdeth their loins with a girdle. He leadeth princes away spoiled, and overthroweth

the mighty. He removeth away the speech of the trusty, and taketh away the understanding of the aged. He poureth contempt upon princes, and weakeneth the strength of the mighty. He discovereth deep things out of darkness, and bringeth out to light the shadow of death. He increaseth the nations, and destroyeth them: he enlargeth the nations, and straiteneth them again. He taketh away the heart of the chief of the people of the earth, and causeth them to wander in a wilderness where there is no way. They grope in the dark without light, and he maketh them to stagger like a drunken man (Job 12:6–25).

Job shares the insight into sojourn wisdom of God with us. He is confident that God is in total control and his wisdom is just toward all matters in heaven and earth. Job spoke these facts in view of his knowledge of God.

An excellent example of the wisdom of God is enveloped in the life story of King Solomon (2 Chr. 1:7–12). We find an overview of how Solomon obtained gifts of wisdom and riches from the Lord. Solomon had gone up to the place where he was to build the tabernacle of the Lord that his father David had promised the Lord that he would build in order to sacrifice unto the Lord. Verses 7-12 reads,

> In that night did God appear unto Solomon, and said unto him, Ask what I shall give thee. And Solomon said unto God, Thou hast shewed great mercy unto David my father, and hast made me to reign in his stead. Now, O LORD God, let thy promise unto David my father be established: for thou hast made me king over a people like the dust of the earth in multitude. Give me now wisdom and knowledge, that I may go out and come in before this people: for who can judge this thy people, that is so great? And God said to Solomon, Because this was in thine heart, and thou hast not asked riches, wealth, or honour,

nor the life of thine enemies, neither yet hast asked long life; but hast asked wisdom and knowledge for thyself, that thou mayest judge my people, over whom I have made thee king: Wisdom and knowledge is granted unto thee; and I will give thee riches, and wealth, and honour, such as none of the kings have had that have been before thee, neither shall there any after thee have the like.

Solomon asked God for wisdom, and Solomon asked not incorrectly or waver in his faith. Solomon is recorded to have been the wisest and richest king who ever lived. He wrote three books of wisdom published in the Holy Bible: Ecclesiastics, Song of Solomon, and Proverbs. These books testify of Solomon's wisdom and wealth:

And God gave Solomon wisdom and understanding exceeding much, and largeness of heart, even as the sand that is on the sea shore. And Solomon's wisdom excelled the wisdom of all the children of the east country, and all the wisdom of Egypt. For he was wiser than all men; than Ethan the Ezrahite, and Heman, and Chalcol, and Darda, the sons of Mahol: and his fame was in all nations round about. And he spake three thousand proverbs: and his songs were a thousand and five. And he spake of trees, from the cedar tree that is in Lebanon even unto the hyssop that springeth out of the wall: he spake also of beasts, and of fowl, and of creeping things, and of fishes. And there came of all people to hear the wisdom of Solomon, from all kings of the earth, which had heard of his wisdom (1 Kings 4:29–34).

I think it is equally important to demonstrate how God gave wisdom to people whom he employed to do a specific task. He imparted wisdom unto men, enabling them development of supernatural ability in their craft. In the days of Moses in the book of Exodus, God gives the spirit of wisdom for the job at hand. He gives it to specific persons. And he will do the same for you if you ask.

> And the LORD spake unto Moses, saying, See, I have called by name Bezaleel the son of Uri, the son of Hur, of the tribe of Judah And I have filled him with the spirit of God, in wisdom, and in understanding, and in knowledge, and in all manner of workmanship, To devise cunning works, to work in gold, and in silver, and in brass, And in cutting of stones, to set them, and in carving of timber, to work in all manner of workmanship. And I, behold, I have given with him Aholiab, the son of Ahisamach, of the tribe of Dan: and in the hearts of all that are wise hearted I have put wisdom, that they may make all that I have commanded thee; The tabernacle of the congregation, and the ark of the testimony, and the mercy seat that is thereupon, and all the furniture of the tabernacle, And the table and his furniture, and the pure candlestick with all his furniture, and the altar of incense, And the altar of burnt offering with all his furniture, and the laver and his foot, And the cloths of service, and the holy garments for Aaron the priest, and the garments of his sons, to minister in the priest's office, And the anointing oil, and sweet incense for the holy place: according to all that I have commanded thee shall they do (Ex. 31:1–11).

God will give you wisdom to perform any work that you cannot do. Another example was the manufacturing of the holy garments for the priesthood, which he himself was the designer of.

> And take thou unto thee Aaron thy brother, and his sons with him, from among the children of Israel, that he may minister unto me in the priest's office, even Aaron, Nadab and Abihu, Eleazar and Ithamar, Aaron's sons. And thou shalt make holy garments for Aaron thy brother for glory and for beauty. And thou shalt speak

unto all that are wise hearted, whom I have filled with the spirit of wisdom, that they may make Aaron's garments to consecrate him, that he may minister unto me in the priest's office. And these are the garments which they shall make; a breastplate, and an ephod, and a robe, and a broidered coat, a mitre, and a girdle: and they shall make holy garments for Aaron thy brother, and his sons, that he may minister unto me in the priest's office. And they shall take gold, and blue, and purple, and scarlet, and fine linen (Ex. 28:1–5).

These craftsmen received the spirit of wisdom from God.

The wisdom of God is imparted to us by communicating with God. We refer to it as revelation. Abiding in Christ produces the wisdom of God. "The fear of the LORD is the beginning of wisdom: and the knowledge of the holy is understanding" (Prov. 9:10). As you commune with the Lord, you will gain revelation into whom he is, which will produce fear (reverence) of him. This is the beginning of true wisdom. The more you study and seek him, the wider the door of knowledge of the Holy One will open to you. As you learn more about God and his ways, the more you will understand the world we now live in and the world to come. You will begin to discern the ways of God from the ways of men. This knowledge will enable you to make sound decisions based on what you know is pleasing to God, thus empowering your walk in the ways of God. "Trust in the LORD with all thine heart; and lean not unto thine own understanding. In all thy ways acknowledge him, and he shall direct thy paths" (Prov. 3:5–6). Walking by faith and not by sight is our target. We are to totally trust in God's wisdom and not our own.

Solomon advises his own son, "My son, if thou wilt receive my words, and hide my commandments with thee; So that thou incline thine ear unto wisdom, and apply thine heart to understanding; Yea, if thou criest after knowledge, and liftest up thy voice for understanding; If thou seekest her as silver, and searchest for her as for hid treasures; Then shalt thou understand the fear of the LORD, and find the knowledge of God. For the LORD giveth wisdom: out of his mouth cometh knowledge and understanding. He layeth up sound wisdom for the righteous: he is a buckler to them that walk uprightly. He keepeth the paths of judgment, and preserveth the way of his saints. Then shalt thou understand righteousness, and judgment, and equity; yea, every good path" (Prov. 2:1–9).

The benefits obtained from receiving the wisdom of God— self-preservation, an understanding of righteousness (morality and ethics), judgment and equity (fairness), and every good path—are worthy of the quest.

Ecclesiastes is an analytical view of the sum of life's aspirations through the eyes of Solomon. He continuously employs one word (vanity) when describing the benefits of accomplishing our material aspirations. "'Vanity of vanities,' says the Preacher, 'Vanity of vanities! All is vanity.' What advantage does man have in all his work which he does under the sun?" (Eccl. 1:2–3). Solomon begins with a conclusion and a question that inspires us to consider what we really have accomplished after applying energy and effort to human laborious projects and undertakings, encouraging thought regarding the purpose of life. Ecclesiastes is, I think, one of the greatest books of philosophy written by one of the wisest, richest men who ever lived. One of the most profound and gifted thinkers takes us into the recesses of his thoughts, unveiling the view from which he ponders human and animal behaviors, natural developments, and God. After that, he forms this conclusion: "Let us hear the conclusion of the whole matter: Fear God, and keep his commandments: for this is the whole duty of man" (Eccl. 12:13).

How do we know we have the wisdom of God or the wisdom of this world? James dives into the answer by presenting a question to his church, which is fighting over the position of wise men. James asks, "Who is a wise man and endued with knowledge among you? let him show out of a good conversation his works with meekness of wisdom. But if ye have bitter envying and strife in your hearts, glory not, and lie not against the truth. This wisdom descendeth not from above, but is earthly, sensual, devilish. For where envying and strife is, there is confusion and every evil work. But the wisdom that is from above is first pure, then peaceable, gentle, and easy to be intreated, full of mercy and good fruits, without partiality, and without hypocrisy. And the fruit of righteousness is sown in peace of them that make peace" (Jas. 3:13–18).

James says that, if we have wisdom, it will be seen in your ability to contain our knowledge in meekness and good conversation. Henry Matthew's commentary writes the exploratory view as such,

> A truly wise man is a very knowing man: he will not set up for the reputation of being wise without laying in a good stock of knowledge; and he will not value himself merely upon knowing things, if he has not wisdom to make a right application and use of that knowledge. These two things must be put together to make up the account of true wisdom: who is wise, and endued with knowledge? Now where this is the happy case of any there will be these following things:—1. A good conversation. If we are wiser than others, this should be evidenced by the goodness of our conversation, not by the roughness or vanity of it. Words that inform, and heal, and do good, are the marks of wisdom; not those that look great, and do mischief, and are the occasions of evil, either in ourselves or others. 2. True wisdom may be known by its works. The conversation here does not refer only to words, but to the whole of men's practice; therefore it is said, Let him show out of a good conversation his works. True wisdom does not lie in good notions or speculations so much as in good and useful actions. Not he who thinks well, or he who talks well, is in the sense of the scripture allowed to be wise, if he do not live and act well. 3. True wisdom may be known by

the meekness of the spirit and temper: Let him show with meekness, etc. It is a great instance of wisdom prudently to bridle our own anger, and patiently to bear the anger of others. And as wisdom will evidence itself in meekness, so meekness will be a great friend to wisdom; for nothing hinders the regular apprehension, the solid judgment, and impartiality of thought, necessary to our acting wisely, so much as passion. When we are mild and calm, we are best able to hear reason, and best able to speak it. Wisdom produces meekness, and meekness increases wisdom.

As we all are aware, most people who have wisdom are not so willing to argue a point, for it is wisdom who nudges them to wait patiently for the show in the doing. If you ask God for his wisdom, he will reveal wisdom to you. Wisdom was there with him from the beginning.

> When wisdom entereth into thine heart, and knowledge is pleasant unto thy soul; Discretion shall preserve thee, understanding shall keep thee: To deliver thee from the way of the evil man, from the man that speaketh froward things; Who leave the paths of uprightness, to walk in the ways of darkness; Who rejoice to do evil, and delight in the frowardness of the wicked; Whose ways are crooked, and they froward in their paths: To deliver thee from the strange woman, even guide of her youth, and forgetteth the covenant of her God. For her house inclineth unto death, and her paths unto the dead. None that go unto her return again, neither take they hold of the paths of life. That thou mayest walk in the way of good men, and keep the paths of the righteous. For the upright shall dwell in the land, and the perfect shall remain in it. But the wicked shall be cut off from the earth, and the transgressors shall be rooted out of it (Prov. 2:10–22).

To show partiality is not good, Because for a piece of bread a man will transgress.
Proverbs 28:21

Chapter 4
Respect of Persons

Temptations to have respect of persons or show partiality among persons will certainly present itself from day one in business. Preferring a person with wealth and resources to a person who is of limited means is the Western civilization's way. The temptation is a great one for every Christian businessman to endure, due to the fact that one of the major reasons you are in business is to obtain the financial freedom to do whatever you want in life. Freedom from the bounds of limited income will afford you freedom in many areas of life. King Solomon says, "A feast is made for laughter, and wine maketh merry: but money answereth all things" (Eccl. 10:19). This is one of Satan's more successful traps that are laid for us. Many Christians have fallen into this one, for the world would advise, that It is wise to take good care of the rich man at all cost because if you find favor in his eyes he can and will give you financial stability and security. This, my friend, is a fallacy, totally unscriptural and definitely untrue. James instructs us on this issue,

> My brethren, have not the faith of our Lord Jesus Christ, the Lord of glory, with respect of persons. For if there come unto your assembly a man with a gold ring, in goodly apparel, and there come in also a poor man in vile raiment; And ye have respect to him that weareth the gay clothing, and say unto him, Sit thou here in a good place; and say to the poor, Stand thou there, or sit here under

my footstool: Are ye not then partial in yourselves, and are become judges of evil thoughts? Hearken, my beloved brethren, Hath not God chosen the poor of this world rich in faith, and heirs of the kingdom which he hath promised to them that love him? But ye have despised the poor. Do not rich men oppress you, and draw you before the judgment seats? Do not they blaspheme that worthy name by the which ye are called? (Jas. 2:1–7)

James tells us that we commit a sin when we treat a person with nice clothes and fine jewelry better than a person with poor hygiene and shabby clothes. He first says that we are not to have faith of Christ coupled with the respect or disrespect of persons. James makes the point that Christ chooses the poor of this world, being rich in faith and love for God, qualifying him to possess the kingdom of heaven, therefore making all men of substance in his sight. If the poor are accepted by God because of his inner riches which gives access to the Kingdom of God, who are we to accept them not. James accuses the Israelites of being partial or biased and judgmental in their hearts. He asks them two questions, encouraging them to think about whom it is that they give this favor to.

> "But ye have despised the poor. Do not rich men oppress you, and draw you before the judgment seats? Do not they blaspheme that worthy name by the which ye are called?" (Jas. 2:6).

He asks his audience to consider the fact that the rich are always taking the poor to court to take from them. Then he draws our attention to the fact that non christians have no respect for our religion or the precious name of Jesus. There is simply no advantage, and it very well may be to our disadvantage to have respect of persons. James then reminds us of the commandments and laws of God: "If ye fulfill the royal law according to the scripture, Thou shalt love thy neighbour as thyself, ye do well: But if ye have respect to persons, ye commit sin, and are convinced of the law as transgressors. For whosoever shall keep the whole law, and yet offend in one point, he is guilty of all" (Jas. 2:8–10).

These are very strong words from James to the church. Obviously, the statement is made to discourage this assembly from the practice.

Moses lays down this law to the Israelite judges: "And I charged your judges at that time, saying, Hear the causes between your brethren, and judge righteously between every man and his brother, and the stranger that is with him. Ye shall not respect persons in judgment; but ye shall hear the small as well as the great; ye shall not be afraid of the face of man; for the judgment is God's: and the cause that is too hard for you, bring it unto me, and I will hear it" (Deut. 1:16–17).

Moses was instructing the judges and leaders that he installed into office over God's people. He commands them, knowing that God is just to all men and his judgment is just. He is speaking from the mind and heart of God. He tells them not to consider the bullying stances and threats of men. They have no authority to judge. The judgment is God's and God's only. He does not want the judges to be persuaded in their judgment by men, small or great.

Jehoshaphat tells the judges that there is no iniquity with the Lord our God, nor respect of persons, nor taking of gifts (2 Chr. 19:7). Deuteronomy 10:17–18 says, "For the LORD your God is God of gods, and Lord of lords, a great God, a mighty, and a terrible, which regardeth not persons, nor taketh reward: He doth execute the judgment of the fatherless and widow, and loveth the stranger, in giving him food and raiment."

First and foremost, the speaker establishes that God is the supreme authority in all the earth, among all the powers that be. He has all power over good and evil powers that exist. He is not a God that takes bribes of any kind. God is uninterested in how much you can give to him in exchange for his respect of your person. He gives blessings and executes judgment the same to all persons without regard for their stature in the earth. If our lawmakers and judges were to adhere to the words of Moses today, the country and the world would be a much better place to live in.

We find an event where the Pharisees, after studying the behavior of Jesus, presented him with a question in an effort to find cause to report him to the law for persecution, which indicated that Jesus did not respect persons. "And when they were come, they say unto him, Master, we know that thou art true, and carets for no man: for thou regards not the person of men, but teaches the way of God in truth: Is it lawful to give tribute to Caesar, or not?" (Mark 12:14).

Surely, the Pharisees would not have paid him this compliment, undeserving of his behavior. They sought to kill him. We, as representatives of Jesus Christ, must follow his example in this the same matter. Jesus had no respect of persons because he knew the hearts of men and that they all sinned in the same manner alike. We should follow his lead, trusting that whatever he was, we do well if we aspire to be.

What of us who sin in and overabundance of self-respect? "And he said unto them, Ye are they which justify yourselves before men; but God knoweth your hearts: for that which is highly esteemed among men is abomination in the sight of God" (Luke 16:15). In fact, earlier in the book of Luke (Luke 14:7–11), Jesus gives us a parable instructing us on how to have humility and warning us of the embarrassment of having to be asked to step down from a place of high esteem. This parable is for us as much as it is for the worldly man.

And he put forth a parable to those which were bidden, when he marked how they chose out the chief rooms;

saying unto them, When thou art bidden of any man to a wedding, sit not down in the highest room; lest a more honourable man than thou be bidden of him; And he that bade thee and him come and say to thee, Give this man place; and thou begin with shame to take the lowest room. But when thou art bidden, go and sit down in the lowest room; that when he that bade thee cometh, he may say unto thee, Friend, go up higher: then shalt thou have worship in the presence of them that sit at meat with thee. For whosoever exalteth himself shall be abased; and he that humbleth himself shall be exalted.

Knowing this, we strive for the approval of God. Humility is what we strive for. If the humbled man shall be exalted by God and is highly esteemed in the eyes of God, which is greater? To have man's honor or the honor of God? To be accepted by God is always better.

The apostle Paul tells the church at Corinth not to judge anything before its time. Instead, we are to wait for the Lord to come, who will then bring the hidden things to light and reveal the inner secrets of the heart. The truth will be told in all things, and we will glorify God. Exalt not even them as their ministers above what the Lord has allowed.

Let a man so account of us, as of the ministers of Christ, and stewards of the mysteries of God. Moreover it is required in stewards, that a man be found faithful. But with me it is a very small thing that I should be judged of you, or of man's judgment: yea, I judge not mine own self. For I know nothing by myself; yet am I not hereby justified: but he that judgeth me is the Lord. Therefore judge nothing before the time, until the Lord come, who both will bring to light the hidden things of darkness, and will make manifest the counsels of the hearts: and then shall every man have praise of God. And these things, brethren, I have in a figure transferred to myself and to

Apollos for your sakes; that ye might learn in us not to think of men above that which is written, that no one of you be puffed up for one against another (1 Cor. 4:1–6).

Behavior of this nature causes misunderstanding and division, not to mention that our judgment is seldom accurate. Let God be the judge.

We must be careful not to judge people by what or who we perceive them to be. We read of the many instances of angelic visitations to the people of God mentioned in Bible. Angels brought messages from God to his people. In many instances, they were sent to the people for protection and guidance. Let it not be said that God could not approach you in this manner because of your inability to accept his method. God will communicate to us in whatever way he chooses. The Old Testament is full of stories that include angels sent from heaven to help us fulfill a set plan of God. There are far too many instances to begin to reference. Hebrews 13:1–3 gives the best advice: "Let brotherly love continue. Be not forgetful to entertain strangers: for thereby some have entertained angels unawares. Remember them that are in bonds, as bound with them; and them which suffer adversity, as being yourselves also in the body."

The author warns us that angels do appear and they don't always reveal their identity. We should always expect God to interact with us. The author then tells us to be mindful of the men and women in prison, keeping in mind that, as long as we are still in the body, we are also subject to worldly afflictions and physical discomforts.

I would finally like to cover racial prejudice. Let us take Acts 10, where God sent Peter to the house of Cornelius, a Centurion of a band called the Italian Ban. He was a devout man and one who feared God with all his house, which gave much alms to the people and prayed to God always. Now, we must understand that the Jewish custom was not to mingle or keep company with other races of people. Through this chapter, God reveals to Peter that he should not call common (unclean) the things that he made clean through his death and resurrection. He simply tells him that the things he has made clean are no longer called common (unclean).

Peter then goes to tell the people, "And he said unto them, Ye know how that it is an unlawful thing for a man that is a Jew to keep company, or come unto one of another nation; but God hath showed me that I should not call any man common or unclean" (Acts 10:28). Acts 10:34–35 says, "Then Peter opened his mouth, and said, Of a truth I perceive that God is no respecter of persons: But in every nation he that feareth him, and worketh righteousness, is accepted with him." His statements abolish the thought of racial bias from the church. If God felt this way concerning race and his church, then surely we should take the same position.

When we typically see the sin of respect of persons being carried out, we can assume that the sinner believes that the person he granted these special privileges to can repay him in some way financially by reciprocating the same privileges or simply giving him honor for the deed. The Lord says through Jeremiah,

> Thus saith the LORD; Cursed be the man that trusteth in man, and maketh flesh his arm, and whose heart departeth from the LORD. For he shall be like the heath in the desert, and shall not see when good cometh; but shall inhabit the parched places in the wilderness, in a salt land and not inhabited. Blessed is the man that trusteth in the LORD, and whose hope the LORD is. For he shall be as a tree planted by the waters, and that spreadeth out her roots by the river, and shall not see when heat cometh, but her leaf shall be green; and shall not be careful in the year of drought, neither shall cease from yielding fruit. The heart is deceitful above all things, and desperately wicked: who can know it? I the LORD search the heart, I try the reins, even to give every man according to his ways,

and according to the fruit of his doings. As the partridge sitteth on eggs, and hatcheth them not; so he that getteth riches, and not by right, shall leave them in the midst of his days, and at his end shall be a fool (Jer. 17:5–11).

First and foremost, a curse means, according to Merriam-Webster's dictionary, "a prayer or invocation for harm or injury to come upon one: imprecation, something that is cursed or accursed, evil or misfortune that comes as if in response to imprecation or as retribution, a cause of great harm or misfortune: torment."

God decrees a curse if man depends on or puts his faith in a person for his support or well-being. Why? God has encouraged us to lean on him and depend on him only all through the Bible. God understands that our fellow men are weak in mind, spirit, and body. He knows men will disappoint you. He doesn't want us to have to depend on undependable beings with limited strength that cannot even save himself. He knew the heart of man, and he says, "Deceitful above all things, and desperately wicked: who can know it?" He asks a question that he already has the answer to. No one can really know the heart of man but God. Who searches the heart? In verse 10, he states, "I the LORD search the heart, I try the reins, even to give every man according to his ways, and according to the fruit of his doings." God judges according to the heart of man and gives everyone what he just deserves. So it doesn't matter what we think. God says you will not get what you do not deserve. We will not unjustly bear hardships stowed upon us or reap the repercussions of another man's sins. He gives us what we justly earn. This means that, even if we try to obtain more of anything that we do not deserve, God will not allow it because he is just. He does not argue the point with us. He weighs the intents of the heart. He knows you. He knows what you meant when you did whatever you did, good or bad.

The final point in this scripture reading tells us what happens to our vain efforts: "As the partridge sitteth on eggs, and hatcheth them not; so he that getteth riches, and not by right, shall leave them in the midst of his days, and at his end shall be a fool." He says that, even though it may appear that you have the object of your desire in your possession, you will not benefit from the object because you obtained it not by right. You took it unlawfully according to God's law. In the end, your work will come to nothing, and you will be a fool.

If you head into business with a mind to give to the client, whom you believe can provide what you need sufficiently, you are headed for disaster. People are masters at hiding their inadequacy from other people, preventing you from judging from a glance. Some people who appear unable to pay for the work you do will be more than able, but some who appear able will be unable. Good advice is to follow the instructions of the Bible: "Have no respect of persons." How will we know if God is God of Gods, Lord of Lords, a great God, a mighty and a terrible God, as Deuteronomy 10:17 states? By placing all of our trust in him for everything. To become totally and utterly dependent on him for everything that pertains to our lives. He will prove himself to be worthy.

*For thou art my rock and my fortress; therefore for
thy name's sake lead me, and guide me.*
Psalms 31:3

Chapter 5
Lead by the Spirit

CONDUCTING BUSINESS WITHOUT CONSULTING GOD and waiting to receive an answer is to proceed at your own risk, especially when you enter into business contracts with other business associates and partners. What might seem to be fairly insignificant decisions, for example, whether or not to hire a certain person or if the time is right to add to your staff, will need comprehensive consideration. You will not find a more knowledgeable advisor then God's spirit or the Holy Spirit. I think this chapter will be of great assistance to you when you are confronted with complicated as well as minimal business matters.

First and foremost, it is important that I provide understanding for what "lead by the spirit" means. What does it mean for the spirit to lead you, and how is it done? In this chapter, I will explain how God leads us by his spirit and how we follow the prompting and leading of the Holy Ghost. Let's get a clear definition of the word "lead." Webster's defines "lead" as precedence; a going before; and guidance. To be led by the spirit simply means to allow the spirit of God to precede or guide you. Now, in order to be led, you must give the spirit the authority to be the leader and look to him for guidance. Let me illustrate what I mean. If you were walking down a street with a busy highway with your child by the hand and you came to a major intersection, would your child take the lead and not expect you to pull him or her back if it were unsafe to cross? No. Children expect their parents to guide them when danger is near. Even animals expect their parents to guide and protect them when encountering danger. Well, God has promised this same protection to his children. "But the Comforter, which is the Holy Ghost, whom the Father will send in my name, he shall teach you all things, and bring all things to your remembrance, whatsoever I have said unto you" (John 14:26). The promise is to teach us all things, everything. Why then would you want to run ahead of the Comforter? He was sent to us to comfort us when we are unsure of the different paths we should take and various decisions we must make in life.

"Peace I leave with you, my peace I give unto you: not as the world giveth, give I unto you. Let not your heart be troubled, neither let it be afraid" (John 14:27). Knowing this, if you find that you do not have peace with a matter and your heart is troubled, then you should refrain from moving forward. You will have the peace of God when God is guiding and abiding with you in all matters. In fact, the Holy Spirit will send you warnings preceded by unrest within your conscience. The word of the Lord will accompany this unrest, verifying the presence of the Holy Spirit. It is he who is causing your distress.

> I will instruct thee and teach thee in the way which thou shalt go: I will guide thee with mine eye. Be ye not as the horse, or as the mule, which have no understanding: whose mouth must be held in with bit and bridle, lest they come near unto thee. Many sorrows shall be to the wicked: but he that trusteth in the LORD, mercy shall compass him about. Be glad in the LORD, and rejoice, ye righteous: and shout for joy, all ye that are upright in heart (Ps. 32:8–11).

Oh, what a solid rock we stand on and in what mighty arms we rest. "He that dwelleth in the secret place of the most High shall abide under the shadow of the Almighty" (Ps. 91:1). Oh, what solace to know that my protection and guidance is under the direct shadow of the creator of the universe, the creator of all things that exist.

Never run ahead of God. Wait on the Lord in conducting your business. Doing business in this world is full of traffic jams and accidents. There are many snares to fall prey to, which were designed just for you, the new business owner. You are green, just green. Believe it or not, you are also a prime target because you're a Christian. You are careful not to hurt anyone's feelings by saying no. God forbid you don't help people. Make it a habit to instantly take everything to God in prayer. He is faithful to answer you in every matter. If you find these sentences repeating themselves in your mind—"This deal is only for today … It will not ever come again … You have to decide now"—you can rest assured that you are being persuaded to do something you might shy away from if you give yourself time to think about it. "A prudent man foreseeth the evil, and hideth himself: but the simple pass on, and are punished" (Prov. 22:3). Have it printed, and put it over your desk in your office. Let your heart fix itself on the following: "Trust in the LORD with all thine heart; and lean not unto thine own understanding. In all thy ways acknowledge him, and he shall direct thy paths" (Prov. 3:5–6). The writer concludes that God's direction will direct our path as a result of our acknowledgement of God.

Now let's talk a bit about receiving guidance from God. Guidance from God is not comingled with the lust of the flesh or desires of our flesh. This guidance is a direct result of walking with and adhering to the unction of the Holy Spirit. Let's consider what Paul says, "This I say then, Walk in the Spirit, and ye shall not fulfil the lust of the flesh. For the flesh lusteth against the Spirit, and the Spirit against the flesh: and these are contrary the one to the other: so that ye cannot do the things that ye would. But if ye be led of the Spirit, ye are not under the law" (Gal. 5:16–18).

If we wish the spirit to lead us, we plainly see here that we are to be subject to the spirit of God. Only then are we not under the law. We must allow our lust to die and allow the Holy Spirit to decide what we will do in our flesh. Further into the text, Paul describes what lusts the flesh caters to. Then he lists attributes of the fruits of the spirit:

Now the works of the flesh are manifest, which are these; Adultery, fornication, uncleanness, lasciviousness, Idolatry, witchcraft, hatred, variance, emulations, wrath, strife, seditions, heresies, Envyings, murders, drunkenness, revellings, and such like: of the which I tell you before, as I have also told you in time past, that they which do such things shall not inherit the kingdom of God. But the fruit of the Spirit is love, joy, peace, longsuffering, gentleness, goodness, faith, Meekness, temperance: against such there is no law. And they that are Christ's have crucified the flesh with the affections and lusts. If we live in the Spirit, let us also walk in the Spirit (Gal. 5:19).

The spirit will lead you if you want to be lead. So says the old saints in my church. The Holy Spirit is a gentle spirit. It will not drag you kicking and screaming to places you don't want to go. Paul states, "This I say therefore, and testify in the Lord, that ye henceforth walk not as other Gentiles walk, in the vanity of their mind, Having the understanding darkened, being alienated from the life of God through the ignorance that is in them, because of the blindness of their heart: Who being past feeling have given themselves over unto lasciviousness (expressing Lust), to work all uncleanness with greediness. But ye have not so learned Christ; If so be that ye have heard him, and have been taught by him, as the truth is in Jesus: That ye put off concerning the former conversation the old man, which is corrupt according to the deceitful lusts; And be renewed in the spirit of your mind" (Eph. 4:17–23).

We are told to renew even the spirit of our minds, to think with the new mind of Christ. How do we do this? Paul draws us a map: "Finally, brethren, whatever things are true, whatever things are noble, whatever things are just, whatever things are pure, whatever things are lovely, whatever things are of good report, if there is any virtue and if there is anything praiseworthy—meditate on these things" (Phil. 4:8).

The renewing of the spirit of your mind happens as a result of the practice of controlling your thoughts. What you allow yourself to think matters. After practice, godly thoughts will come naturally.

And that ye put on the new man, which after God is created in righteousness and true holiness. Wherefore putting away lying, speak every man truth with his neighbour: for we are members one of another. Be ye angry, and sin not: let not the sun go down upon your wrath: Neither give place to the devil. Let him that stole steal no more: but rather let him labour, working with his hands the thing which is good, that he may have to give to him that needeth. Let no corrupt communication proceed out of your mouth, but that which is good to the use of edifying, that it may minister grace unto the hearers. And grieve not the holy Spirit of God, whereby ye are sealed unto the day of redemption. Let all bitterness, and wrath, and anger, and clamour, and evil speaking, be put away from you, with all malice: And be ye kind one to another, tenderhearted, forgiving one another, even as God for Christ's sake hath forgiven you (Eph. 4:24–32).

Your moral character and spiritual posture will become your identity.

We come into God's presence via prayer, meditation, and fasting. Employing these methods, he draws us near to him. When we are drawn close to God, you may then expect and are in a position to receive his divine guidance. Answers from God will come in various ways. The Lord will speak to you through your spirit, unvailing revelation and imparting new and necessary information to you. "But the manifestation (public demonstration) of the Spirit is given to each one for the profit of all: for to one is given the word of wisdom through the Spirit, to another the word of knowledge through the same Spirit" (1 Cor. 12:7–8).

Some will argue that these gifts are given only to certain people and God uses them in the same capacity every time they manifest. I beg to differ. I believe that God is precise and he gives us what we need when we need it. One way that God speaks to us is through the written word of God, the Bible. "All Scripture is given by inspiration of God, and is profitable for doctrine, for reproof, for correction, for instruction in righteousness" (2 Tim. 3:16).

God also uses our dreams. But I have a word of caution with your dreams. If the dream does not line up with the way the Bible instructs us to walk before God and leads us away from God, then he did not send the dream to you.

> If there arises among you a prophet or a dreamer of dreams, and he gives you a sign or a wonder, and the sign or the wonder comes to pass, of which he spoke to you, saying, "Let us go after other gods—which you have not known—and let us serve them," you shall not listen to the words of that prophet or that dreamer of dreams, for the Lord your God is testing you to know whether you love the Lord your God with all your heart and with all your soul. You shall walk after the Lord your God and fear Him, and keep His commandments and obey His voice, and you shall serve Him and hold fast to Him (Deut. 13:1–4).

You must learn to discern between good and evil, although there is evidence throughout the Bible proving that God reveals many things to us through dreams. For example, Joseph had a dream predicting he would be a ruler in Egypt (Gen. 37). When the journey before us will be hard, tedious, and challenging, God will sometimes give us a sneak preview to let us know that he has ordered our steps and he will be there through the hard places. Nebuchadnezzar, the king of Babylon, dreamt of future events concerning his kingdom, and Daniel interpreted them for him (Dan. 2).

So God uses dreams as a form of communication. Often, God will use symbols in dreams. Sometimes, they are very easy to understand, but at times, you will be left puzzled. But in due season, as you watch events unfold, God will help you to understand the dream. It is safe to say, whenever you have a dream, you should ask God for the interpretation.

Visions are also one of God's avenues of communication to his people. The word "vision" means something seen in a dream or a trance to foreseeing or foresight. We are sometimes given the answer through visualization or imagination. Visions often follow fasting, prayer, and lamentation, coupled with the setting apart of oneself unto God. Daniel was in mourning for three weeks before he received his answer. He fasted and did not groom himself during this time (Dan. 10:2). Daniel was praying when Gabriel came to give him skill and understanding of a vision he had experienced (Dan. 9:20–23). We do get some answers from God through visions. The book of Daniel is full of knowledge concerning visions.

When seeking God, don't be surprised if God chooses to send you one of his messengers. When you are a child of God, there is nothing too good for you. God gave us, the body of Christ, prophets for edification to help us to grow into the fullness of our new nature in Christ. "Now you are the body of Christ, and members individually. And God has appointed these in the church: first apostles, second prophets, third teachers, after that miracles, then gifts of healings, helps, administrations, varieties of tongues" (1 Cor. 12:27–28). Why?

For the equipping of the saints for the work of ministry, for the edifying of the body of Christ, till we all come to the unity of the faith and of the knowledge of the Son of God, to a perfect man, to the measure of the stature of the fullness of Christ; that we should no longer be children, tossed to and fro and carried about with every wind of doctrine, by the trickery of men, in the cunning craftiness of deceitful plotting, but, speaking the truth in love, may grow up in all things into Him who is the head—Christ—from whom the whole body, joined and knit together by what every joint supplies, according to the effective working by which every part does its share, causes growth of the body for the edifying of itself in love (Eph. 4:12–16).

This is one of the benefits of being part of the family of Christ. Be diligent and watchful to ensure that you receive, believe, and act on the word when it comes. Beware when receiving a word of prophecy.

And it shall come to pass, that whosoever will not hearken unto my words which he shall speak in my name, I will require it of him. But the prophet, which shall presume to speak a word in my name, which I have not commanded him to speak, or that shall speak in the name of other gods, even that prophet shall die. And if thou say in thine heart, How shall we know the word which the LORD hath not spoken? When a prophet speaketh in the name of the LORD, if the thing follow not, nor come to pass, that is the thing which the LORD hath not spoken, but the prophet hath spoken it presumptuously: thou shalt not be afraid of him (Deut. 18:19–22).

Remember the following:
- All of the written word is true.
- If the word of the prophet does not come to pass, the word was not from God.

Wait for God. The Lord will confirm his word to you. He will confirm it in two or three ways or through two or three people. If you receive a word from the Lord and a contradictory word comes forth to you from God, always follow what you receive directly from the Lord. If God chooses to change the path of your walk, wait for a confirmation of the word you are acting on, whether it is directly from him or a prophet. For example, there is a story about a man of God in 1 Kings 13:1. This story is one of a man of God who got a word of instruction from Lord. He was to cry out against a false alter that Jeroboam had built in Bethel. The man of God obeyed and the sign which the Lord had spoken to him was fulfilled. The sign from the Lord was that the alter shall be rent, and the ashes that are upon it shall be poured out. These events came to pass. God had also told the prophet that he was not to go into the house of the king, nor to eat bread or drink water in the place. This man of God was overheard by an old prophets' sons. They repeated this conversation to their father. The old prophet invited him over to his home to be refreshed. The man of God repeated the instructions to him from the Lord, not to eat or drink in that place. After identifying himself, the old prophet then lied to him. He said that an angel spoke unto him by the word Lord saying bring him into his house and he may then eat and drink. The man of God followed him home, he drank and ate . As he sat at bread God passed judgment and punishment because he did not keep the commandment that the Lord gave him. There are a few lessons to learn in this story that will help you be obedient and careful.

1. God prohibited eating and drinking of this messenger in Bethel to show his hatred of the kings apostasy from God. God is discouraging fellowship with the works of darkness. By fellowshipping with darkness we are infected by it or we give encouragement to it.

2. When we do not obey God we put ourselves at risk of being devoured by self preservation. I am convinced that hunger and thirst, our basic physical needs may tempt us to relinquish the word of the Lord to our own detriment.

3. Don't receive a word from God from other people that is contrary to the word that you yourself received

from the Lord. Every spirit is not of God. John warns us to try the spirits in 1John 4:1 as is illustrated in the story.

As your walk purifies you with the Lord, you will receive direction from him. Don't worry that you might not recognize the voice of God. Jesus said, "My sheep hear My voice, and I know them, and they follow Me" (John 10:27).

Sometimes God does not give us the answers that we desire. When this happens, you must receive the truth and understand that what Isaiah 55:8 states is also true: "'For My thoughts are not your thoughts, Nor are your ways My ways,' says the Lord." And Paul reminds us, "Oh, the depth of the riches both of the wisdom and knowledge of God! How unsearchable are His judgments and His ways past finding out! For who has known the mind of the Lord? Or who has become His counselor? Or who has first given to Him and it shall be repaid to him? For of Him and through Him and to Him are all things, to whom be glory forever. Amen" (Rom. 11:33–36).

What God decides is truly best for us is best. So if God chooses a path in your life that does not appear to be what you thought it should be, just know we have to trust him because he is the guide.

Most of us fall because we believe we can do business without the guidance of God. When God guides us into a situation, he will provide for us the grace to successfully get through or the anointing to conquer it. The word "anointing" literately means to ordain or consecrate. When we receive God's grace to go through a problem, you will find yourself basking in the peace of God throughout the situation. On the other hand, when you receive the anointing to conquer, you will be confident of the power God provides for you to go in and win the battle. You will know that you have obtained the help of God because the outward appearance of the situation looks impossible. The impossible yokes are broken (snapped) by the anointing. God's anointing breaks the yokes.

In the book of Isaiah, there is an example of the voice of God during a very desperate period in Elijah's life when he prayed for himself and his safety. We should look to this example to see how God answered him.

Elijah had four hundred of Jezebel's prophets killed, and he was running for his life. After journeying for days, he reached Horeb, the mountain of God, where he prayed and anxiously awaited the answer. During his wait, he carefully searched the environment and atmosphere for the answer. He was unsure of how God would answer. He made sure he was attentive as to not miss the message from God. Many events occurred in the atmosphere that summons his attention, but it was not God. The King James Version of the Bible records the story:

> Then He said, "Go out, and stand on the mountain before the Lord." And behold, the Lord passed by, and a great and strong wind tore into the mountains and broke the rocks in pieces before the Lord, but the Lord was not in the wind; and after the wind an earthquake, but the Lord was not in the earthquake; and after the earthquake a fire, but the Lord was not in the fire; and after the fire a still small voice (1 Kings 19:11–12).

God spoke to him in a still small voice. Uh, still small voice. Sounds familiar? Elijah looked for God to speak to him in a spectacular way, as most of us do. God chose to speak in a quiet little voice. Because God is a god, we tend to expect him to shake the earth when he speaks. This story is our evidence that God doesn't always enter the room with splendor and glory or catastrophe. God is sojourn. He answers and enters our space as he will. Sometimes he speaks to us in a still small voice or perhaps in the cool of the day. "And they heard the voice of the LORD God walking in the garden in the cool of the day: and Adam and his wife hid themselves from the presence of the LORD God amongst the trees of the garden" (Gen. 3:6–8).

Oh, that we have not a reason for camouflage when God speaks to us. When the day is done, the business is closed, and you thought your customer was coming in to pick up the item and pay for it but didn't, you've already paid for the item. He is known for speaking to us

- after the church service is over and nobody prophesied to you about your situation,
- when you have returned from the conference and still cannot sort things out,
- when you've talked out your problems to everybody you know and still can't see God in the answers, and
- when you exhausted all your options.

Then God speaks. I often think he is waiting for us to just be quiet so he may talk to us.

And last but not least, with a tender, gentle, caring arm, God guides us through carved-out paths that lead to places that are set aside especially for us. He is careful not to injure or scare us along the way. Evidence of this truth is found in Exodus. God leads the people out of Egypt, careful to take them on a safe route. "Now when Pharaoh had let the people go, God did not lead them by the way of the land of the Philistines, even though it was near; for God said, 'The people might change their minds when they see war, and return to Egypt'" (Ex. 13:22).

Hence, God led the people around by the way of the wilderness to the Red Sea, and the sons of Israel went up in martial array from the land of Egypt. Moses took the bones of Joseph with him, for he had made the sons of Israel solemnly swear, saying, "God will surely take care of you, and you shall carry my bones from here with you." Then they set out from Succoth and camped in Etham on the edge of the wilderness. The Lord was going before them in a pillar of cloud by day to lead them on the way and in a pillar of fire by night to give them light so they might travel by day and by night. He did not take away the pillar of cloud by day nor the pillar of fire by night from before the people. God was mindful of their present condition.

Enslavement by a cruel taskmaster embedded feebleness of mind, apprehension of revolt, and fear of failure in them, which intensified through the generations. He had great mercy and compassion when bringing them out. So with us, he knows where and when we are weak. He is faithful to go before us to lead us in the way and give us light to see the way.

I would finally like to share one last verse. "Thus sayeth the LORD, thy Redeemer, the Holy One of Israel; I am the LORD thy God which teacheth thee to profit, which leadeth thee by the way that thou shouldest go" (Isa. 48:17). He has made his position known to us, and he will do that which he has promised. He will teach us to profit as he leads us by the way.

For as he thinketh in his heart, so is he.
Proverbs 23:7

Chapter 6

Guard Your Heart

I WROTE THIS CHAPTER TO help you understand how utterly imperative it is that your heart is kept. "Keep your heart with all diligence, For out of it spring the issues of life" (Prov. 4:23). The word "keep" causes my mind to allude to a scenic view of a flower garden. We till, plant, fertilize, water, and weed a garden to encourage what has been planted to grow into its full beauty and valor for us to admire. We prevent various weeds from taking over. We keep away grubs that destroy and eat the plant roots. We defend our plants from animals who feed on them after they have blossomed. The gardener works to prevent the flowers from going through a premature death.

When we plant a seed, if it is a good one, beautiful brilliant flowers, luscious fruits, or vividly colored vegetables will sprout from it. During the growing process, we soon discover other very aggressive wild roots grow under the earth that just naturally grow alongside our plants. These will wrap themselves around the root of the plant and strangle it to death. It is not the gardener's fault that the weeds spring up, for the gardener did not plan them. All the same, it is imperative that the farmer pull them out to ensure the livelihood of his garden. We must till our soil every year in preparation for the new seeds to ensure a good crop. So as it is with the heart, it's kind of like a garden. We must search our hearts daily for weeds that may spring up through the night and pull them out by the root. "The heart is deceitful above all things, And desperately wicked; Who can know it? I, the Lord, search the heart, I test the mind, Even to give every man according to his ways, According to the fruit of his doings" (Jer. 17:9–10).

Guard your heart, and be very careful about the things you allow to grow in it. We will be rewarded according to our doings. Jesus explains the subject of heart issues: "But those things which proceed out of the mouth come from the heart, and they defile a man. For out of the heart proceed evil thoughts, murders, adulteries, fornications, thefts, false witness, blasphemies. These are the things which defile a man, but to eat with unwashed hands does not defile a man" (Matt. 15:18–20).

He tells us that the mouth speaks whatever is in the heart, which leads to violations of the law in the spirit and then in the flesh. First, the heart and then the mind begin to cultivate evil thoughts. This is where we can correct it. Be instantaneous with correcting what's in the heart. It's not what you do outwardly that causes you to be evil in your heart. It is first conceived in the heart. Your actions then follow. Actions are the result of thoughts. That's where the saying "Actions speak louder than words" comes from. James explains it like this: "Let no one say when he is tempted, 'I am tempted by God'; for God cannot be tempted by evil, nor does He Himself tempt anyone. But each one is tempted when he is drawn away by his own desires and enticed. Then, when desire has conceived, it gives birth to sin; and sin, when it is full-grown, brings forth death" (Jas. 1:13–15).

Where are these desires conceived? In the heart. We must be careful with the heart. All sin starts first in the heart of a man, and then it works its way to the outward acts of each human being. A good example of selfishness harbored within us is outward acts of greed, covertness, and stinginess. Selfishness plays such a great part in ushering in more sin. We must beware of what we are bargaining for when we do not keep our hearts. Let me echo James here: "Then, when desire has conceived, it gives birth to sin; and sin, when it is full-grown, brings forth death." When we allow various sins to dwell in our hearts, it affects the people around us. Whatever is in our hearts is what we have to touch other people's lives with, whether it is love and understanding or self-centeredness and hatefulness. The Lord holds us accountable for what we allow to linger in our hearts. When we allow our hearts to build up a rock-hard core of protection, we can't feel what other people feel. This rocky core has a built-in layer that shields us from caving in emotionally during the turbulent storms of life, but it also prevents us from having heartfelt compassion. The compassion of God, without which a man can truly serve, robs us of the ability to touch another man's experience with the understanding obtained from an experience of our very own. We are protected from emotions meant to be harvested from particular experiences that have happened in our own lives to make us strong. Events, good and bad, build character and encourage endurance that simulate and challenge our inner child, forcing it into adulthood. Our hearts are designed to feel.

I recall an incident when anger lingered in my heart. I refused to forgive a customer. A customer had come into my store a few weeks before Christmas for repair to her ten-year-old computer. She explained her dilemma to me. Her daughter was on the honor roll, and she wanted the computer fixed to present it to her on Christmas Day. I leaped at the opportunity to help. I took my own personal money from my pocket to buy the parts. I rushed everybody: the parts vendors and the engineer preforming the repair. There was also the anxiety I experienced over the whole idea of helping a poor honor student get back on track for the next semester of school. I was obsessed with making the deadline, the night before Christmas. The business account was running a little low. The parts came to several hundred dollars, which I so willingly took from my own children's Christmas money. After all, I knew this customer was going to be in to pick up this computer. We were to close on Christmas Eve in celebration of the birth of Jesus Christ. The day before Christmas Eve came. Nobody picked up the computer. It was all repaired and clean. I got up the next day and opened up the store just for her. Nobody showed. I was left with absolutely no money on Christmas Eve and no toys. At approximately 6:00 p.m. that evening, I had nothing close to what I spent on that repair. I was angry. As a matter of fact, I still have an old Apple computer that I can't give away. She never even bothered to call back or return our calls for that matter. I ran into her often at the grocery store, hair salon, and community activities. I knew her personally. I had broken one of my own store policies for her, never begin a job without payment for the parts. I had to eventually forgive the customer because it was affecting my ability to have compassion for other customers who came in with direr and pressing issues. The community I served needed compassion and accommodation. That was the least I could do. I looked at my heart.

People will try to make money from your business. They will try multiple methods of securing a financial profit from your venture. Doing business today is more challenging than ever before in that there are new and innovative ways to do business, but these new avenues also invite thieves to swindle from you. The names of games, along with the rules, are changed. The games that people play in Africa are played on the people in the United States. The games that people in China had to watch out for, people in Italy will fall prey to. The Internet makes you more vulnerable. You can advertise and sell all over the world. You have also become instantaneous prey for the world. I love the Internet. It great for information, but it is truly the Wild Wild West out there. There are no international laws that will discourage or prevent thieves from stealing your bank accounts or your products. Be careful. With this wealth of information at our fingertips, we gain knowledge, and we are tempted to pursue more. Desire is increased, and dreams are pumped up to tremendous heights. We have to watch what we allow to overwhelm and oversaturate our hearts.

The world is becoming increasingly evil. We must remember what the apostle Paul instructs us to do about others injuring us. "Repay no one evil for evil. Have regard for good things in the sight of all men. If it is possible, as much as depends on you, live peaceably with all men. Beloved, do not avenge yourselves, but rather give place to wrath; for it is written, 'Vengeance is Mine, I will repay,' says the Lord. Therefore If your enemy is hungry, feed him; If he is thirsty, give him a drink; For in so doing you will heap coals of fire on his head. Do not be overcome by evil, but overcome evil with good" (Rom. 12:17–21).

With that, I can say that we should know that God judges, promotes, and demotes us by what is in our hearts. "But the LORD said unto Samuel, Look not on his countenance, or on the height of his stature; because I have refused him: for the LORD seeth not as man seeth; for man looketh on the outward appearance, but the LORD looketh on the heart" (1 Sam. 16:7–13).

The word "countenance" means composure, face, or expression. The Lord, when choosing a king from the house of Jessie, instructed Samuel not to choose a king by looking at his outward appearance. His mannerisms, ability to speak properly, good looks, or facial expressions were all off the table. None of it was important because God looked deeper than the surface when choosing him for his work. So it is with us, He looks and then appoints us according to the condition of our hearts.

David asked the Lord to re-create his heart: "Create in me a clean heart, O God; and renew a right spirit within me. Do not cast me away from Your presence, And do not take Your Holy Spirit from me. Restore to me the joy of Your salvation, And uphold me by Your generous Spirit. Then I will teach transgressors Your ways, And sinners shall be converted to You" (Ps. 51:10).

He has concluded that the only chance of redemption is if two issues are addressed within himself:

- His heart is completely re-created or reconstructed.
- His spirit is renewed within himself.

He knows that only God can perform this kind of work within one's soul and spirit. With this re-creation of heart, he plans to win souls to Christ. David is correct to assume that he is equipped to teach transgressors the ways of Lord under the condition that the work on himself is completed.

Not slothful in business; fervent in spirit; serving the Lord.
Romans 12:11

Chapter 7
Discipleship and Business

DISCIPLESHIP IS A CAPTIVATING BUT paramount ingredient that is thrown into the mix in business. Many Christians are leery about mixing Christianity with business, but it comes with the territory. Public interaction permits the study of your character. Whether it's running a business, teaching a classroom full of kids, or working in customer service, human services, social service, and so forth, wherever you find yourself in your world, there will your character be as well. I say "your world" because we, as human beings, through the process of evolution, form our own little worlds in which we live. These worlds that we create are expanded only when compelled by forced circumstances or some other form of force, such as God. Business gives you great opportunities to influence people from all walks of life. You have access to the homeless man on the street, presidents of corporations, and sometimes presidents of countries. It is important to understand that, with such exposure, you will be able to authentically change the course in the lives of many. The stage will be yours. The opportunity to transform another person's life will be tremendous. People will either be motivated and turn to the God you serve or discouraged from serving your God.

The Pauline Gospels are richly sprinkled with effective techniques that can be employed when winning various nationalities and ethnic groups to Christ. The apostle Paul outlines his method so plainly for us. "For though I am free from all men,

I have made myself a servant to all, that I might win the more; and to the Jews I became as a Jew, that I might win Jews; to those who are under the law, as under the law, that I might win those who are under the law; to those who are without law, as without law (not being without law toward God, but under law toward Christ), that I might win those who are without law; to the weak I became as weak, that I might win the weak. I have become all things to all men, that I might by all means save some. Now this I do for the gospel's sake, that I may be partaker of it with you" (1 Cor. 9:19–23).

Paul simply says that he makes it a point to serve all men. His objective is to draw as many people to Christ as he deemed utterly possible in his lifetime. He plans to use the art of persuasion by first knowing (studying) his subject. He observes the traditions and cultures of people that he runs across for the sole purpose of winning them to Christ. Then he "became as" the people he encountered in order to win them over to Christ, disregarding the state he finds them in. What an excellent idea. Christians are often unsuccessful at evangelizing due to our approach and distorted view of nonbelieving people. If they were already saved and living their lives unto the glory of God, they have no need of you. True evangelism is to minister to a person with whom you have absolutely nothing in common. Jesus demonstrated this same technique in the book of Mark and his purpose for using it to the Scribes and the Pharisees. "And when the scribes and Pharisees saw Him eating with the tax collectors and sinners, they said to His disciples, 'How is it that He eats and drinks with tax collectors and sinners?' When Jesus heard it, He said to them, 'Those who are well have no need of a physician, but those who are sick. I did not come to call the righteous, but sinners, to repentance'" (Mark 2:16–17).

You should not reject people because of their differences in behavior. You will have the greatest influence on these people. The ultimate goal is the end result, bringing the person into the knowledge of God. Their transformation will occur through time and spiritual growth. Your business is the best platform to do this from. In business, you have direct access and opportunity to make an impression on the general public. The same is true of the public concerning you. It is vital that you perform what is civil, ethical, and morally correct in business. The public will be viewing you. You can use so many proverbs and sayings from the wisdom books in the Bible that will aid in your personal efforts to improve your moral character. People of all ages are like children in that they do what they see you do and not what they hear you say. They very rarely stand still long enough to hear what you are saying. If they are standing still, they are most likely not intensely listening to what you are saying. If you're trying to sell something that you yourself are not investing in, they have already decided to dismiss it on the grounds that you didn't buy it yourself. Therefore, you don't believe in the stock. Actions do speak louder than you do. People are apt to be influenced by what they see you do that is enriching to the mind, body, and spirit. They have to get something out of what they welcome into their lives. If things are not working out for you and don't look good on you, like you're bouncing checks written to suppliers or sharing your nasty attitude with the customers, don't expect other people to want to try it on themselves. You must practice what you preach. You will not have to say a word if you live it out.

Your testimony will be your life. Funerals always bring a story with them. Some are lonely and sad, summoning only a few poor souls to share reflections of the life the deceased has exited. Others draw hundreds of people to celebrate the life you are entering into. Write your story as you live, while encourageing other people to do the same. A life that has been lived unto God will be celebrated even in death. Only you can write your story. God's intent was that you live the life he gave you to it's fullest with one inclusion, himself.

In order to be a disciple in business, you must be sensitive and mindful of what the Bible says our appearance should be to other people. It is important to understand that, with such exposure, your message will be broadcasted to the community at large. You will have an audience. The opportunity to transform another person's life will be tremendous. People will either become motivated and turn to the God you serve or become discouraged from serving your God. People study what you do, and most have little respect for hypocrites. Jesus himself so stated: "Woe to you, scribes and Pharisees, hypocrites! For you are like whitewashed tombs which on the outside appear beautiful, but inside they are full of dead men's bones and all uncleanness" (Matt. 23:27). Who you really are is transparent to people. Nobody respects a fake. A call for intimacy with God is first initiated through a realization of utter emptiness that spotlights the need of something deep down within the soul that is missing. They should be able to study you and see that you are whole, lacking nothing. It's almost impossible to help people obtain something that you yourself have not yet obtained. How can you lead people to water when you don't know where it is yourself? So the best way to disciple in business is to lead by example. It works.

Assisting God with spiritual births can be closely compared to the human birthing process. Timing is everything to God. God alerts his staff and prepares for delivery according to the timing that the mother's body naturally sets itself up. He relies on the natural process of the events before beckoning his crew to assist in the delivery. There he waits. During this period, he checks to make sure that all the tools and supplies are promptly available to him that would assist him in assuring the patient of a safe and successful delivery. All the surgical tools are laid out on a tray within his reach. He is the authority in high-risk pregnancies and deliveries.

Bringing a baby into the family is no easy task for the mother especially. A number of ground rules need to be established, and because the mother is more familiar with this new member, the weight of smooth transition into the family is on her shoulders. First, she must make sure the baby has all his essential needs met. The child's emotional needs must also be met, which the mother takes responsibility for. Everyone must cater to the newborn. No one is permitted to dislike the baby because the baby cannot yet defend himself. His place in the family is established on the day he arrives. Everyone is secondary to the baby in all things. When the baby cries, everybody listens to see who's attending the baby. The new mother is on edge, making sure everything is perfect for the new family member. She instructs everyone to speak softly as to allow the baby a proper amount of sleep. She demands that the baby is handled gently, ensuring that no harm is unintentionally caused. She wants the baby's clothes always clean for ultimate comfort, encouraging cleanliness in the child's life. She demands all the family members respect the child's infancy period of growth, at least until it is of age to defend itself in some ways. This is the job of the evangelist. You should take an active role in the development of the spiritual babies that you have assisted with their entrance into the world.

The apostle Paul states, "For no other foundation can anyone lay than that which is laid, which is Jesus Christ. Now if anyone builds on this foundation with gold, silver, precious stones, wood, hay, straw, each one's work will become clear; for the Day will declare it, because it will be revealed by fire; and the fire will test each one's work, of what sort it is. If anyone's work, which he has built on, it endures, he will receive a reward. If anyone's work is burned, he will suffer loss; but he himself will be saved, yet so as through fire" (1 Cor. 3:11–15).

Paul compares this work to building a structure. He makes an analogy to a building being constructed. The differences is the materials we use. He begins first with the foundation, Jesus Christ, which shall hold up the structure. The foundation is the strongest part of the building. Without it, the building will begin to crack and fall. Foundations are usually made of concrete. He mentions that our work will be tried, rendering a telling verdict. The trials of life will be your fire, exposing the strength of your structure. This demonstrates and then substantiates reasons why you should build with certain types of materials. The saving grace lies in the fact that it may suffer damage but will be saved ultimately.

So in retrospect, there are a few points to keep in the mind and heart in business. First, people are watching your behavior and listening to little of what you say. You are influencing people through your actions.

But be doers of the word, and not hearers only, deceiving yourselves. For if anyone is a hearer of the word and not a doer, he is like a man observing his natural face in a mirror; for he observes himself, goes away, and immediately forgets what kind of man he was. But he who looks into the perfect law of liberty and continues in it, and is not a forgetful hearer but a doer of the work, this one will be blessed in what he does (Jas. 1:22–25).

Be tolerant, patient, long-suffering, and accommodating. People will be more apt to accept and embrace you and your ideas if you accept and embrace them and theirs. Be attentive and instrumental in the birthing process. The new baby needs your help. And last but not least, lay no other foundation that which was laid, which is Jesus Christ.

But let patience have her perfect work, that ye may be perfect and entire, wanting nothing.
James 1:4

Chapter 8
Patience through Knowing

WE MUST ACQUIRE PATIENCE. IT is derived through knowing and experiencing the nature of God. You will discover in business, as well as all other aspects of your existence in this world, that God is in control of all of your circumstances and he knows how much you can bear. "For he shall give his angels charge over thee, to keep thee in all thy ways. They shall bear thee up in their hands, lest thou dash thy foot against a stone" (Ps. 91:11–12). Thus, you will soon learn in business that your greatest disappointments and disasters will be the avenues God uses to reveal his mind and heart to you. The tools you think you must have on board to ensure the success of your business, loans, contracts, contacts, and special employees will be where God proves to you what he says. "'For My thoughts are not your thoughts, Nor are your ways My ways,'" declares the LORD. For [as] the heavens are higher than the earth, So are My ways higher than your ways And My thoughts than your thoughts" (Isa. 55:8–9). This will turn out to be truth. He can see much further down the road than we can, as my grandfather Willie T. Smith used to say. He is omniscient. He is all knowing and everywhere at all times, always ready to lead and guide our every footstep to reveal his chosen pathway to us. He guides us lovingly down his paths with precision, knowing what each individual traveler will need to finish his journey. "I will instruct you and teach you in the way you should go; I will guide you with My eye" (Ps. 32:8). God promises through the meditations of David that he will use his own eye to guide us. Having God give us the benefit of his vision, his sharpness, and perception is an awesome advantage to go through life in possession of. He uses his own sight, his view, to guide us, and because he guides us through the paths he envisions for our lives, we cannot get lost along the way. He sustains us with food and water at appointed rest areas on the trip, if need be. He even commands the fowls of the air to bring us food.

And Elijah the Tishbite, of the inhabitants of Gilead, said to Ahab, "As the Lord God of Israel lives, before whom I stand, there shall not be dew nor rain these years, except at my word." Then the word of the Lord came to him, saying, "Get away from here and turn eastward, and hide by the Brook Cherith, which flows into the Jordan. And it will be that you shall drink from the brook, and I have commanded the ravens to feed you there." So he went and did according unto the word of the LORD: for he went and dwelt by the brook Cherith, that is before Jordan. And the ravens brought him bread and flesh in the morning, and bread and flesh in the evening; and he drank of the brook (1 Kings 17:1–6).

The Lord commanded the birds of the air to bring his breakfast and dinner. How distinct and specifically designed are the pathways themselves to aid in the perfecting and strengthening of his journeyman. God knows the way that he would have us to go, and if we stay on the path that he prepares for us, we are sure to finish our course without frustration or exhaustion.

As for the day-to-day stresses we will experience, the apostle James has some good advice: "My brethren, count it all joy when ye fall into divers temptations; knowing that the trying of your faith worketh patience. But let patience have her perfect work, that ye may be perfect and entire, wanting nothing" (Jas. 1:2–4). He implies that, without the challenging of your faith, there cannot be a perfect work of patience in you. Therefore, patience is perfected through the testing of your faith.

The word "patience" means *hupomone* in Greek, or cheerful (or hopeful) endurance, consistency, enduring, patience, and patient continuance (waiting). The apostle Paul weighs in, saying, "Therefore, being justified (admissible) by faith, we have peace with God through our Lord Jesus Christ: by whom also we have access by faith into this grace wherein we stand, and rejoice in hope of the

Glory of God. And not only so, but we glory in tribulations also: knowing that tribulation worked patience; and patience, experience; and experience hope: and hope market not ashamed; because the love of God is shed abroad in our hearts by the Holy Ghost which is given unto us" (Rom. 5:1–6).

Paul tells us here that tribulation (misfortune, trials, and sufferings), worked patience (endurance and continuance), and patience produces experience (knowledge, skill, and practice) and experience, which then formulates hope (confidence, chance, desire, and want) in us. Then he says that hope makes us not ashamed. Why? Our hope (confidence) is in God and his direction during tribulations.

Patience (endurance) is an essential component necessary for spiritual development and the element that strengthens our hope (confidence) in the Lord. We learn through our tribulation that God is faithful to show us that he is always there to help and guide us through.

Watching the miraculous arm of the Lord move in our behalf, we develop patience (endurance) in knowing (experience). Knowing without a doubt that God is with you and he has never left you alone at any of those times when you thought you were in trouble, in need of divine intervention in your circumstances, and though you could not feel or see his hand on your shoulder, he was directing the orchestra at your concert. Hallelujah! Glory to the Divine Director! God is to be glorified in all things. Apostle Paul says, "And we know that all things work together for the good of them that love God, and that who are the called according to his purpose" (Rom. 8:28). With this confidence, we can have patience in knowing that God is working out all things for our own ultimate good and, in business, all things will work out for the good. We can have patience that he is faithful to transform all of our bad or poorly-thought-out decisions into the most needed and appropriate ideas.

Patience is the reward we receive after we have grown past the place of knowing!

But thou shalt remember the LORD thy God: for it is he that giveth thee power to get wealth, that he may establish his covenant which he sware unto thy fathers, as it is this day.
Deuteronomy 18

Chapter 9
Wealth through God's Eye

TIMOTHY UTTERS, "FOR THE LOVE of money is the root of all evil: which while some coveted after, they have erred from the faith, and pierced themselves through with many sorrows" (1 Tim. 6:10). He fervently warns his parishioners concerning the love of money. Love of money is the sin here. People may have money and not love it, but the love of it will persuade you to do unthinkable acts to obtain it. He warns that the pursuit (chase) of it, in the past and future, will cause one to fall away from the faith. The fervor of the chase demands that you give up the faith pending the completion of it. Prior to the statement, Timothy professes, "But godliness with contentment is great gain. For we brought nothing into this world, and it is certain we can carry nothing out. And having food and raiment let us be therewith content. But they that will be rich fall into temptation and a snare, and into many foolish and hurtful lusts, which drown men in destruction and perdition" (1 Tim. 6:6–9).

He inspires the people within his audience by saying that godliness and contentment is great gain. Without either, we are unhappy. He points out that we cannot take anything with us into the grave. This is, I believe, one of the most familiar scriptures in the Bible. Some use it to justify their own personal poverty; others use it to reprimand those who have obtained wealth. This scripture is also often used as a tool of manipulation. They have adopted a "if you are poor then, you are holy" type of philosophy, suggesting that environmental and economic poverty proves your willingness to sacrifice everything to God. When we suggest this, we overlook the fact that God is interested in the inner man. Outer appearances are stately but within your inner being is where the sacrifice is offered. Jesus said it best: "Woe to you, scribes and Pharisees, hypocrites! For you cleanse the outside of the cup and dish, but inside they are full of extortion and self-indulgence. Blind Pharisee, first cleanse the inside of the cup and dish, that the outside of them may be clean also. Woe to you, scribes and Pharisees, hypocrites! For you are like whitewashed tombs which indeed appear beautiful outwardly, but inside are full of dead men's bones and all uncleanness. Even so you also outwardly appear righteous to men, but inside you are full of hypocrisy and lawlessness" (Matt. 23:25–28).

Jesus warns against promoting outside cleansing of the body for the purpose of appearances while leaving the inner man unclean for righteousness is from the inside out. Our outside appearances cannot and will not determine righteousness.

Timothy spoke of the love of money to simply help Christians control their lust for money and material things, which will impede their faith over time. He witnessed that this particular desire compelled people to do anything to obtain it, including abandoning their faithfulness to God and the church. He was simply trying to convince his people to have money but not let money have them. After all, they needed money to purchase food and raiment, not to mention supporting the church. God himself did not intend to allow his people to believe that their own hands could make him wealthy. The proof lies in Deuteronomy 8:10–20:

> When thou hast eaten and art full, then thou shalt bless the LORD thy God for the good land which he hath given thee. Beware that thou forget not the LORD thy God, in not keeping his commandments, and his judgments, and his statutes, which I command thee this day: Lest when

thou hast eaten and art full, and hast built goodly houses, and dwelt therein; And when thy herds and thy flocks multiply, and thy silver and thy gold is multiplied, and all that thou hast is multiplied; Then thine heart be lifted up, and thou forget the LORD thy God, which brought thee forth out of the land of Egypt, from the house of bondage; Who led thee through that great and terrible wilderness, wherein were fiery serpents, and scorpions, and drought, where there was no water; who brought thee forth water out of the rock of flint; Who fed thee in the wilderness with manna, which thy fathers knew not, that he might humble thee, and that he might prove thee, to do thee good at thy latter end; And thou say in thine heart, My power and the might of mine hand hath gotten me this wealth. But thou shalt remember the LORD thy God: for it is he that giveth thee power to get wealth, that he may establish his covenant which he sware unto thy fathers, as it is this day.

In this statement, I am persuaded that God's intention was to bless the people of Israel with great wealth in honoring the covenant he made with Abraham, the father of our faith. But in doing so, he also made them aware of the temptation to forget how they obtained the blessing, thus saying in their own hearts, "My power and the might of mine hand hath gotten me this wealth." He makes it clear that he only gave them the power to get wealth, why "that he may establish his covenant which he sware unto thy fathers, as it is this day."

Let us look at the covenant God made with Abraham to try to understand just what God views were regarding wealth and blessing and how this covenant transpired, which covered all the sons of Abraham.

In Genesis 15:18, we find a formal covenant between God and Abraham. Before a formal covenant was drafted, God made promises and oaths to Abraham during the call of Abraham by God. This promise (covenant) was made after Abraham was obedient to God's command to leave his father's house with his wife and go to a land that God would show him.

> Now the LORD had said unto Abram, Get thee out of thy country, and from thy kindred, and from thy father's house, unto a land that I will show thee: And I will make of thee a great nation, and I will bless thee, and make thy name great; and thou shalt be a blessing: And I will bless them that bless thee, and curse him that curseth thee: and in thee shall all families of the earth be blessed (Gen. 12:1–3).

This was the first time that God spoke to Abram about his future fame and the great nation of people that would be procreated by him.

- The first promise was Abraham's fame and the procreation of a great nation. As Abram (High Father) obeyed God, God continued to communicate to Abraham about his welfare and the welfare of his seed. "And the LORD appeared unto Abram, and said, Unto thy seed will I give this land: and there builded he an altar unto the LORD, who appeared unto him. And he removed from thence unto a mountain on the east of Bethel, and pitched his tent, having Bethel on the west, and Hai on the east: and there he builded an altar unto the LORD, and called upon the name of the LORD" (Gen. 12:7–8).
- The second promise from God was land (property) designated for his children. After which, Abram began to worship God. He built an altar unto the Lord and called on the name of the Lord. Now Genesis 13, we find that Abram is very rich at this point. Abraham had journeyed down into Egypt. He got in trouble with Pharaoh, God cursed Pharaoh to get him out of

Egypt, and Abraham left the country. Abraham then went back to Bethel, where he built an altar and called again on the name of the Lord. "And Abram was very rich in cattle, in silver, and in gold. And he went on his journeys from the south even to Bethel, unto the place where his tent had been at the beginning, between Bethel and Hai; Unto the place of the altar, which he had made there at the first: and there Abram called on the name of the LORD" (Gen. 13:2–4). Abraham had Lot with him. The two men were so rich with material possessions that they could not dwell together. Genesis 13:5–6 tells this fact: "And Lot also, which went with Abram, had flocks, and herds, and tents. And the land was not able to bear them, that they might dwell together: for their substance was great, so that they could not dwell together." I am led to believe that God blessed Abraham and Lot so much that they were forced to spread out over the land. God's provision is always more than we expect. It always surpasses what we can envision. Does God bless his people with wealth? With great joy he does.

- The third promise came as a result of Abraham complaining to God that God had given him no heir and all his wealth would have to go to one person born in his house. God then promised him a seed from his own bowels. Being near one hundred years old, Abraham believed God and counted it to him for righteousness. "After these things the word of the LORD came unto Abram in a vision, saying, Fear not, Abram: I am thy shield, and thy exceeding great reward. And Abram said, Lord GOD, what wilt thou give me, seeing I go childless, and the steward of my house is this Eliezer of Damascus? And Abram said, Behold, to me thou hast given no seed: and, lo, one

> born in my house is mine heir. And, behold, the word
> of the LORD came unto him, saying, This shall not
> be thine heir; but he that shall come forth out of thine
> own bowels shall be thine heir. And he brought him
> forth abroad, and said, Look now toward heaven,
> and tell the stars, if thou be able to number them:
> and he said unto him, So shall thy seed be. And he
> believed in the LORD; and he counted it to him for
> righteousness" (Gen. 15:1–6).

God blessed Abraham with a son shortly thereafter. A formal covenant was performed because Abraham asked God a question. "And he said unto him, I am the LORD that brought thee out of Ur of the Chaldees, to give thee this land to inherit it. And he said, Lord GOD, whereby shall I know that I shall inherit it?" (Gen. 15:7–8).

Abraham wanted a sign or something more than a verbal promise. The formal covenant was then performed according to ancient custom between Abraham and God, involving the cutting in half of sacrificial victims and the two parties passing between them. This was a ceremony where God alone passed through them because only God could carry it out. The covenant was then established. "In the same day the LORD made a covenant with Abram, saying, Unto thy seed have I given this land, from the river of Egypt unto the great river, the river Euphrates: The Kenites, and the Kenizzites, and the Kadmonites, the Hittites, and the Perizzites, and the Rephaims, And the Amorites, and the Canaanites, and the Girgashites, and the Jebusites" (Gen. 15:18–21).

God drew out the exact terms of the contract. He outlined the region of land and named the nations of people who the Israelites would overthrow. Through this one patriarch, we are able to see where God stands on the issue of wealth. He is a willing participant in ensuring blessings for his people, spiritual and material. These promises were made to Abraham but set up to expand well over four hundred years as intended to be extended to all of us as well. They are actually passed down to us through the Abrahamic covenant. This covenant was given to all those who believed. Galatians 3:6–18 states,

> Just as Abraham "believed God, and it was accounted to him for righteousness." Therefore know that only those who are of faith are sons of Abraham. And the Scripture, foreseeing that God would justify the Gentiles by faith, preached the gospel to Abraham beforehand, saying, "In you all the nations shall be blessed." So then those who are of faith are blessed with believing Abraham. For as many as are of the works of the law are under the curse; for it is written, "Cursed is everyone who does not continue in all things which are written in the book of the law, to do them." But that no one is justified by the law in the sight of God is evident, for "the just shall live by faith." Yet the law is not of faith, but "the man who does them shall live by them." Christ has redeemed us from the curse of the law, having become a curse for us (for it is written, "Cursed is everyone who hangs on a tree"), that the blessing of Abraham might come upon the Gentiles in Christ Jesus, that we might receive the promise of the Spirit through faith. Brethren, I speak in the manner of men: Though it is only a man's covenant, yet if it is confirmed, no one annuls or adds to it. Now to Abraham and his Seed were the promises made. He does not say, "And to seeds," as of many, but as of one, "And to your Seed," who is Christ. And this I say, that the law, which was four hundred and thirty years later, cannot annul the covenant that was confirmed before by God in Christ, that it should make the promise of no effect. For if the inheritance is of the law, it is no longer of promise; but God gave it to Abraham by promise.

Abraham believed God, which was accounted to him for righteousness by God. This being the case, Abraham became the father of the faithful. Paul would have us to know that those who are of the faith, believing in Jesus Christ and that he fulfilled the law on Calvery, are the children of Abraham not according to our flesh, but according to the promise; and, that we being the children of Abraham, are justified in the same way that he was. Abraham was justified by faith. Thus the promise made to Abraham (Gen. 12:3), In thee shall all nations be blessed. We have access to all the blessings of God that were promised to Abraham God has justified the heathen world in the way of faith; and therefore in Abraham, the seed, which is in Christ, not the Jews only, but the Gentiles also. Paul calls preaching the gospel to Abraham; and thence infers (v. 9) that those who are of faith, that is, true believers, of what nation soever they are, are blessed with faithful Abraham. Abraham the father of the faithful, by the promise made to him, and therefore by faith as he was. It was through faith in the promise of God that he was blessed, and it is only in the same way that others obtain this privilege. Paul reinarates the facts that if we be in Christ then the abundant life that Abraham lived is also offered to us for the taking. This is our inheritance. God will be for us that are living in the faith and by the commandments of God. Our property, our finances, our families and our souls are all prospered and protected in the hands of Jesus Christ because of the righteousness and promises of Abraham. We who are in business and in Christ are only to look to Abraham to discover the blessings that God has in store for us. Because Abraham was rich in faith God gave him riches in all aspects of his life. Every venture was blessed. So it is with us who are in Christ.

Galatians 3:19–29 says,

What purpose then does the law serve? It was added because of transgressions, till the Seed should come to whom the promise was made; and it was appointed through angels by the hand of a mediator. Now a mediator does not mediate for one only, but God is one. Is the law then against the promises of God? Certainly not! For if there had been a law given which could have given life, truly righteousness would have been by the law. But the Scripture has confined all under sin, that the promise by faith in Jesus Christ might be given to those who believe. But before faith came, we were kept under guard by the law, kept for the faith which would afterward be revealed. Therefore the law was our tutor to bring us to Christ, that we might be justified by faith. But after faith has come, we are no longer under a tutor. For you are all sons of God through faith in Christ Jesus. For as many of you as were baptized into Christ have put on Christ. There is neither Jew nor Greek, there is neither slave nor free, there is neither male nor female; for you are all one in Christ Jesus. And if you are Christ's, then you are Abraham's seed, and heirs according to the promise.

The covenant between God and Abraham applies to all believers today, for we have been included through our faith in Jesus Christ. Therefore, I must say that God will bless whom he will bless and he does not want nor does he need our permission to do it. He makes the following bold statement:

> I will take no bullock out of thy house, nor he goats out of thy folds. For every beast of the forest is mine, and the cattle upon a thousand hills. I know all the fowls of the mountains: and the wild beasts of the field are mine. If I were hungry, I would not tell thee: for the world is mine, and the fullness thereof. Will I eat the flesh of bulls, or drink the blood of goats? Offer unto God thanksgiving; and pay thy vows unto the most High: And call upon me in the day of trouble: I will deliver thee, and thou shalt glorify me (Ps. 50:9–15).

God does not need anything we have, because it's all his. Everything is his. He would never depend on us to feed him. So when we praise him it's for us. He puts his praise in us and then he allows us to speak it out so that we will know who he is.

God instructs us to give him thanks, pay our vows (promises), and then call upon him when we get into trouble. It doesn't matter what kind it is. He can and will deliver us. He will deliver us so completely that we will glorify (worship, deify, or adore) him. Wealth is a gift that is God's to give . We as Christian busnessmen and women can expect that God will bless us so that we will glorify him.

> "Praise ye the LORD. Blessed is the man that feareth the LORD, that delighteth greatly in his commandments. His seed shall be mighty upon earth: the generation of the upright shall be blessed. Wealth and riches shall be in his house: and his righteousness endureth for ever. Unto the upright there ariseth light in the darkness: he is gracious, and full of compassion, and righteous. A good man sheweth favour, and lendeth: he will guide his affairs with discretion" (Ps. 112:1–5).

This was David's view. Solomon states his opinion on the matter: "Behold that which I have seen: it is good and comely for one to eat and to drink, and to enjoy the good of all his labour that he taketh under the sun all the days of his life, which God giveth him: for it is his portion. Every man also to whom God hath given riches and wealth, and hath given him power to eat thereof, and to take his portion, and to rejoice in his labour; this is the gift of God. For he shall not much remember the days of his life; because God answereth him in the joy of his heart" (Eccl. 5:18–20).

Soloman says that it is good to enjoy the things that we can afford as a result of our employment until the day we leave this world. He says that it was God who gives us what we have. Soloman says that riches and wealth that we have are given to us by God. He affirms that we will not remember much of our life when reminiscing over it because God has answered us in the joy of our hearts. Implying that in our ladder days we find ourselves satisfied and content with what God has done. Solomon believed that wealth was a gift from God, which the recipient should enjoy. Taking into consideration what the Bible reveals about wealth, we must conclude that the Lord takes pleasure in providing wealth and prosperity for his people. God holds no alliance with lack. He is a creator, a multiplier and rewards those who diligently seek him. He delights in supplying us with provision

Finally, my brethren, be strong in the Lord,
and in the power of his might.
Ephesians 6:10

Chapter 10
Finally, Brethren

THERE IS AN ABSOLUTE TRUTH that I would like to present to you in this last and final chapter. It is definitely a noteworthy and significant fact. Our God has all authority and power over heaven and Earth, the whole universe at large, to put it simply. I think it's important that we examine who God is. Everything in the universe and all the laws of the universe obey and bow down before him. When I say this, I think of the total compilation of centuries and decades of documentation filled with scientific study and research conducted by men. Numerous expeditions and explorations were and are performed in quest of knowledge. The seekers are anxious to lay claim on a fragment of wisdom unlocking the hidden secrets of the formation and functioning of the universe and everything in it. For example, the laws of gravity (Sir Isaac Newton), Kepler's laws of planetary motion, and laws of physics, kinematics, and dynamics, yes, he created and has dominion over all of it. He designed and implemented the mechanics of how everything in this universe functions, and he seizes control of it whenever he wants to. He demonstrated his power when he turned the sundial back in the midst of battle for Joshua. Let Kepler try to explain this one. Joshua tells the story in Joshua 10:12–14,

> Then Joshua spoke to the LORD in the day when the LORD delivered up the Amorites before the sons of Israel, and he said in the sight of Israel, "O sun, stand still at

Gibeon, And O moon in the valley of Aijalon." So the
sun stood still, and the moon stopped, Until the nation
avenged themselves of their enemies. Is it not written in
the book of Jashar? And the sun stopped in the middle of
the sky and did not hasten to go [down] for about a whole
day. There was no day like that before it or after it, when
the LORD listened to the voice of a man; for the LORD
fought for Israel.

Various scientific and literary sources have proposed many
explanations, such as the slowing or stopping of the Earth on its
axis, a special refraction of the sun's ray prolonging daylight, or
prolonging of darkness (solar eclipse or hailstorm) so the battle
might be fought in the shade. In my opinion, the best explanation
is that the event was a miracle.

First and foremost, he is the creator of all things. While
interrogating Job, God reveals his own credentials and establishes
his sovereign authority in the process. He challenged Job after Job
presumed to know what God will and will not do. Job 38:1–3
says,

> Then the LORD answered Job out of the whirlwind and
> said, "Who is this that darkens counsel By words without
> knowledge? "Now gird up your loins like a man, And I
> will ask you, and you instruct Me!" He says to Job, if you
> know so much about me and what I will and will not do,
> prepare to give me some answers

God makes Job aware of his lack of knowledge of the world
in which he lives. One that he did not create. He reveals to Job
the fact that his counsel is blemishes because of his ignorance.
He then puts Job on the stand to cross examine him, knowing
the answers to the questions that he will ask. His point is to
make Job aware of his sightlessness. He and only God knows
the secrets of his ways. God requires Job to assume the position
of physical strength, and courage. We like Job must not assume

we know what God will do for us in business, it will be to our own demise. We do not have the answers to our dilemmas nor do we have the ability to open the doors of heaven and pour ourselves out blessings. We limit the business' earnings, expansion and growth. We are in the classroom. The nature of business is always changing and we must be open to these changes to stay competitive. God and is the ruler of the whole world order. The state of the world is in his hands. All of our answers remain in God. God humbles Job by awakening and introducing him to vast amounts of specific information he does not know. And so it is with us. When God has to join the conversation or situation to rectify it, our correction is always first.

Job 38:4–24 continues,

Where were you when I laid the foundation of the earth? Tell [Me] if you have understanding, Who set its measurements? Since you know. Or who stretched the line on it? "On what were its bases sunk? Or who laid its cornerstone, When the morning stars sang together And all the sons of God shouted for joy? "Or [who] enclosed the sea with doors When, bursting forth, it went out from the womb; When I made a cloud its garment And thick darkness its swaddling band, And I placed boundaries on it And set a bolt and doors, And I said, Thus far you shall come, but no farther; And here shall your proud waves stop? Have you ever in your life commanded the morning, [And] caused the dawn to know its place, That it might take hold of the ends of the earth, And the wicked be shaken out of it? It is changed like clay [under] the seal; And they stand forth like a garment. From the wicked their light is withheld, And the uplifted arm is broken. Have you entered into the springs of the sea Or walked in the recesses of the deep? Have the gates of death been revealed to you, Or have you seen the gates of deep darkness? Have you understood the expanse of the earth? Tell [Me] if you know all this. Where is the way to the dwelling of light? And darkness, where is its place, That you may take it to its territory And that you may discern the paths to its home? You know, for you were born then, And the number of your days is great! Have you entered the storehouses of the snow, Or have you seen the storehouses of the hail, Which I have reserved for the time of distress, For the day of war and battle? Where is the way that the light is divided, [Or] the east wind scattered on the earth?

God steps in for one reason, to declare his own sovereignty. In business we are not to assume that we know what is going to transpire everyday and that we have all the knowledge we require to ensure our own success. Only God knows how he will command nature to aide us. He knows the limits that he has set over the elements of the earth for today and everyday. God establishes the fact that he created all things, from the naturals elements of the world to and has full rein over them. If it rains or snows today he commands it. When he does command it his purposes are fulfilled though the very act of it. Vegetation and animals are nourished by it and the earth drinks of it. It is safe to say, "if God wills, I will do such and such......". We know not what God will do with the creations he has made.

Job 38:25–41 states, Who has cleft a channel for the flood, Or a way for the thunderbolt, To bring rain on a land without people, [On] a desert without a man in it, To satisfy the waste and desolate land And to make the seeds of grass to sprout? Has the rain a father? Or who has begotten the drops of dew? From whose womb has come the ice? And the frost of heaven, who has given it birth? Water becomes hard like stone, And the surface of the deep is imprisoned. Can you bind the chains of the Pleiades, Or loose the cords of Orion? Can you lead forth a constellation in its season, And guide the Bear with her satellites? Do you know the ordinances of the heavens, Or fix their rule over the earth? Can you lift up your voice to the clouds, So that an abundance of water will cover you? Can you send forth lightnings that they may go And say to you, "Here we are"? Who has put wisdom in the innermost being Or given understanding to the mind? Who can count the clouds by wisdom, Or tip the water jars of the heavens, When the dust hardens into a mass And the clods stick together? Can you hunt the prey for the lion, Or satisfy the appetite of the young lions, When they crouch in [their] dens [And] lie in wait in [their] lair? Who prepares for the raven its nourishment when its young cry to God And wander about without food?

God informs Job that he cares for portions of the earth that men have yet to discover. He handles the issues that we have absolutely no knowledge of. He cares for the parched and dry places of the earth. These questions are presented to Job in a way to reveal to Job his own ignorance and shortsightedness. He shows him his impotency and weaknesses. We are to wise acknowledge our inability to appropriately care of everything. We know so little of what is required for the job. God has divine providence over all. We do not have the means to adequately feed the beasts of the fields or the birds of the air. "God's feeding the fowls, especially these fowls (Matt. vi. 26), is an encouragement to us to trust him for our daily bread. See here, (1.) What distress the young ravens is often in: *They wander for lack of meat.* The old ones, they say, neglect them, and do not provide for them as other birds do for their young: and indeed those that are ravenous to others are commonly barbarous to their own, and unnatural. What they are supposed to do in that distress: They *cry,* for they are noisy clamorous creatures, and this is interpreted as crying to God. It being the cry of nature, it is looked upon as directed to the God of nature. The putting of so favourable a construction as this upon the cries of the young ravens may encourage us in our prayers, though we can but cry, *Abba, Father.*" (Matthew Henry's Commentary pg 734)

We can depend on God to supply all our needs in our homes as well as my business. Understanding and excepting this fact will lighten our burdens tremendously.

Job 39:1–12 states,
Do you know the time the mountain goats give birth? Do you observe the calving of the deer? Can you count the months they fulfill, Or do you know the time they give birth? They kneel down, they bring forth their young, They get rid of their labor pains. Their offspring become strong, they grow up in the open field; They leave and do not return to them. Who sent out the wild donkey free? And who loosed the bonds of the swift donkey, To whom I gave the wilderness for a home And the salt land for his dwelling place? He scorns the tumult of the city, The shoutings of the driver he does not hear. He explores the mountains for his pasture And searches after every green thing. Will the wild ox consent to serve you, Or will he spend the night at your manger? Can you bind the wild ox in a furrow with ropes, Or will he harrow the valleys after you? Will you trust him because his strength is great And leave your labor to him? Will you have faith in him that he will return your grain And gather [it from] your threshing floor?

Job 39:13–18 states,
The ostriches' wings flap joyously With the pinion and plumage of love, For she abandons her eggs to the earth And warms them in the dust, And she forgets that a foot may crush them, Or that a wild beast may trample them. She treats her young cruelly, as if [they] were not hers; Though her labor be in vain, [she] is unconcerned; Because God has made her forget wisdom, And has not

given her a share of understanding. When she lifts herself on high, She laughs at the horse and his rider.

Job 39:19–25 states,
Do you give the horse [his] might? Do you clothe his neck with a mane? Do you make him leap like the locust? His majestic snorting is terrible. "He paws in the valley, and rejoices in [his] strength; He goes out to meet the weapons. He laughs at fear and is not dismayed; And he does not turn back from the sword. The quiver rattles against him, The flashing spear and javelin. With shaking and rage he races over the ground, And he does not stand still at the voice of the trumpet. As often as the trumpet [sounds] he says, "Aha!" And he scents the battle from afar, And the thunder of the captains and the war cry.

Job 39:26–30 states,
Is it by your understanding that the hawk soars, Stretching his wings toward the south? Is it at your command that the eagle mounts up And makes his nest on high? On the cliff he dwells and lodges, Upon the rocky crag, an inaccessible place. From there he spies out food; His eyes see [it] from afar. His young ones also suck up blood; And where the slain are, there is he.

As God has created the hawk with strong and mighty wings to soar and the eagle to make his nest on high, so it is with us. The instinct to earn a living for the support of our families are from God. It is him who has given us the power and strength to succeed. "Our Saviour refers to this instinct of the eagle, Matt. xxiv. 28. *Wheresoever the carcase is, there will the eagles be gathered together.* Every creature will make towards that which is its proper food; for he that provides the creatures their food has implanted in them that inclination. These and many such instances of natural power and sagacity in the inferior creatures, which we cannot account for, oblige us to confess our own weakness and ignorance and to give glory to God as the fountain of all being, power, wisdom, and perfection." (Matthew Henry's Commentary)

He then asks Job, "Will the faultfinder contend with the Almighty?" He refers to himself as the Almighty, the omnipotent (all-powerful), omnipresence (ever-present), omniscience (all-knowing), Supreme Being, and God himself. The question is not what we can do with God. But rather, what can we do without him?

He is also a Deliverer, a Savior. God's maneuvers and acts of heroisms are beyond predictability. We never know what to expect when faced with an impossible situation. He blesses our storehouses and blesses all the works of our hands, then he gives us other blessings from his good treasure. God protects and delivers us in unimaginable ways. King Darius found this out when he had Daniel thrown into the lion's den. The presidents and princes of the kingdom tried to get rid of Daniel. They plotted to find something against him concerning the laws of his God. God was faithful to take charge of the situation by sending his angel to shut the mouths of the lions. Daniel 6:18–24 tells the story,

> Then the king went off to his palace and spent the night fasting, and no entertainment was brought before him; and his sleep fled from him. Then the king arose at dawn, at the break of day, and went in haste to the lions' den. When he had come near the den to Daniel, he cried out with a troubled voice. The king spoke and said to Daniel, "Daniel, servant of the living God, has your God, whom you constantly serve, been able to deliver you from the lions?" Then Daniel spoke to the king: "O king, live forever! My God sent His angel and shut the lions' mouths and they have not harmed me, inasmuch as I was found innocent before Him; and also toward you, O king, I have committed no crime." Then the king was very pleased and gave orders for Daniel to be taken up out of the den.

So Daniel was taken up out of the den and no injury whatever was found on him, because he had trusted in his God. The king then gave orders, and they brought those men who had maliciously accused Daniel, and they cast them, their children and their wives into the lions' den; and they had not reached the bottom of the den before the lions overpowered them and crushed all their bones.

Daniel who was appointed president over a hundred and twenty Princes in the kingdom of Darius the Median, suffered persecution as a result of his deep commitment to God. Jealousy inspired the staff he lorded over him to plot against him. Prayer three times a day was outlawed in which he faithfully indulged himself. They could find no fault in him. The Bible says that Darius promoted Daniel into his position because "he had an excellent spirit in him." Suffering persecution as a result of our faith is something we all will be faced with at one time or another in business. We see here that Daniel was delivered by faithful God from the lion's den. We are not to be afraid of what affliction we suffer for Christ, his deliverance is on the way. Paul wittenssed in 2 Timothy 3:10:

> But thou hast fully known my doctrine, manner of life, purpose, faith, longsuffering, charity, patience, Persecutions, afflictions, which came unto me at Antioch, at Iconium, at Lystra; what persecutions I endured : but out of them all the Lord delivered me. Yea, and all that will live godly in Christ Jesus shall suffer persecution .

We will suffer persecutions because of our faith in Christ Jesus but like Paul we can know that God is faithful to deliver us of them all.

Time will not allow me to refer to all the instances listed in the Bible of his deliverances. Take my word for it. He is a formidable foe to his enemies, a deliverer to his people, a very present help in our trouble. Many of his works are documented for reminisce and reference, for example:

- protecting Noah from the flood (Gen. 8:1–22)
- delivering Lot from a wicked city destroyed by God (Gen. 19:29–30)
- saving Jacob from the fury of his brother after stealing the birthright (family infighting) (Gen. 33:1–16)
- delivering Israel from slavery after four hundred and thirty years (Exodus 12: 29-42
- delivering David from the government (King Saul) (1 Sam. 23:1–29)
- saving the apostle Paul from venomous snake poison (Acts 28:5)
- saving Paul and Silas from jail (Acts 16:25–34)
- saving Israel in battle (Josh. 10:8–11)

And the most significant act was delivering man from the power of darkness in Colossians 1:13. The list goes on.

He also is a provider. These blessings are conditional; that is, they are contingent (dependent) upon us obeying the voice of God and observing and keeping all his commandments. How will we know what he commands? His commandments are written in the word of God (Holy Bible) and in our hearts by the Holy Spirit.

And it shall come to pass, if thou shalt hearken diligently unto the voice of the LORD thy God, to observe and to do all his commandments which I command thee this day, that the LORD thy God will set thee on high above all nations of the earth: And all these blessings shall come on thee, and overtake thee, if thou shalt hearken unto the voice of the LORD thy God. Blessed shalt thou be in the city, and blessed shalt thou be in the field. Blessed shall be the fruit of thy body, and the fruit of thy ground, and the fruit of thy cattle, the increase of thy kine, and the flocks of thy sheep. Blessed shall be thy basket and thy store. Blessed shalt thou be when thou comest in, and blessed shalt thou be when thou goest out. The LORD shall cause thine enemies that rise up against thee to be smitten before thy face: they shall come out against thee one way, and flee before thee seven ways. The LORD shall command the blessing upon thee in thy storehouses, and in all that thou settest thine hand unto; and he shall bless thee in the land which the LORD thy God giveth thee. The LORD shall establish thee an holy people unto himself, as he hath sworn unto thee, if thou shalt keep the commandments of the LORD thy God, and walk in his ways. And all people of the earth shall see that thou art called by the name of the LORD; and they shall be afraid of thee. And the LORD shall make thee plenteous in goods, in the fruit of thy body, and in the fruit of thy cattle, and in the fruit of thy ground, in the land which the LORD sware unto thy fathers to give thee. The LORD shall open unto thee his good treasure, the heaven to give the rain unto thy land in his season, and to bless all the work of thine hand: and thou shalt lend unto many nations, and thou shalt not borrow. And the LORD shall make thee the head, and not the tail; and thou shalt be above only, and thou shalt not be beneath; if that thou hearken unto the commandments of the LORD thy God, which I command thee this day, to observe and to do them: And thou shalt not go aside from any of the words which I command thee this day, to the right hand, or to the left, to go after other gods to serve them (Deut. 28:1–14)

Moses declares here that if the Israelites obey God and do the commandments and not turn to the right or the left meaning, superstition or profaneness. Moses then specifically includes going after other Gods to worship them, God will provide for their outward concerns. He states that blessings will overtake them. These blessing are ours whether we are established in the city or the countryside. His blessing will be a comfort on our trips coming in or going out. What more can be given to us? We have been given the blessing of wealth in our businesses, and that we will lend and not borrow (we export more than we import). We will be the lender and not the debtor. This means that we will earn more than we spend. We will have excess. Weighing in with financial lending institutions.

Matthew Henry's Commentary offers its perspective on God's promises to bless our land and livestock, and on the blessings of our storehouses, and blessings in all the works of our hands. "A blessing is promised, First, On all they had without doors, corn and cattle in the field (v. 4, v. 11), their cows and sheep particularly, which would be blessed for the owners' sakes, and made blessings to them. In order to this, it is promised that God would give them rain in due season, which is called his good treasure (v. 12), because with this river of God the earth is enriched, Ps. 65:9. Our constant supplies we must see coming from God's good treasure, and own our obligations to him for them; if he withhold his rain, the fruits both of the ground and of the cattle soon perish. Secondly, On all they had within doors, the basket and the store (v. 5), the store-houses or barns, v. 8. When it is brought home, God will bless it, and not blow upon it as sometimes he does, Hag. 1:6, Hag. 1:9 . We depend upon God and his blessing, not only for our yearly corn out of the field, but for our daily bread out of our basket and store, and therefore are taught to pray for it every day. [4.] They should have success in all their employments, which would be a constant satisfaction to them: "The Lord shall command the blessing (and it is he only that can command it) upon thee, not only in all thou hast, but in all thou doest, all that thou settest thy hand to," v. 8. This intimated that even when they were rich they must not be idle, but must find some good employment or other to set their hand to, and God would own their industry, and bless the work of their hand (v. 12)." Blessings over the fruit our bodies (bearing and the prosperity of our children), We will be the head and not the tail. We will be above only and never beneath. Making us the leaders and followers in our communities. Strive to take possession of your inheritance today. Receiving these blessing in our lives and our businesses require that we comply with (or act in accordance) to the commandments of God. We must walk uprightly before God, serving him only. Turning not to the right or the left.

So let us take some good advice that Paul so powerfully wrote in a letter to the church at Ephesus:

> Finally, my brethren, be strong in the Lord, and in the power of his might. Put on the whole armor of God, that ye may be able to stand against the wiles of the devil. For we wrestle not against flesh and blood, but against principalities, against powers, against the rulers of the darkness of this world, against spiritual wickedness in high places. Wherefore take unto you the whole armor of God, that ye may be able to withstand in the evil day, and having done all, to stand. Stand therefore, having your loins girt about with truth, and having on the breastplate of righteousness; And your feet shod with the preparation of the gospel of peace; Above all, taking the shield of faith, wherewith ye shall be able to quench all the fiery darts of the wicked. And take the helmet of salvation, and the sword of the Spirit, which is the word of God: Praying always with all prayer and supplication in the Spirit, and watching thereunto with all perseverance and supplication for all saints (Eph. 6:10–18).

We cannot be strong in our own might, for we are but flesh and blood, so he says, "Be strong in the Lord, and the power of the Lord's might," wherein we are capable of standing. He implies that the act of standing will require more strength than man is spiritually and physically endowed with. What we will be challenged to fight against in this world, the wiles of the devil, being alone, we cannot overthrow. The wiles (tricks, deceit, charm) of the devil are spiritual assaults. Aimed to influence and defraud us, trap and ensnare us, into giving up our faith in God. He affirms that, by merely and singularly using the strength of

God, we can stand against these present powers. The powers that Paul points to in his text are explained and so clearly defined for us in the Matthew Henry Commentary:

"For we wrestle not against flesh and blood, etc., v. 12. The combat for which we are to be prepared is not against ordinary human enemies, not barely against men compounded of *flesh and blood,* nor against our own corrupt natures singly considered, but against the several ranks of devils, who have a government which they exercise in this world. (1.) We have to do with a subtle enemy, an enemy who uses wiles and stratagems, as v. 11. He has a thousand ways of beguiling unstable souls: hence he is called a serpent for subtlety, an old serpent, experienced in the art and trade of tempting. (2.) He is a powerful enemy: *Principalities,* and *powers,* and *rulers.* They are numerous, they are vigorous; and rule in those heathen nations which are yet in darkness. The dark parts of the world are the seat of Satan's empire. Yea, they are usurping princes over all men who are yet in a state of sin and ignorance. Satan's is a kingdom of darkness; whereas Christ's is a kingdom of light. (3.) They are spiritual enemies: *Spiritual wickedness in high places,* or wicked spirits, as some translate it. The devil is a spirit, a wicked spirit; and our danger is the greater from our enemies because they are unseen, and assault us ere we are aware of them. The devils are wicked spirits, and they chiefly annoy the saints with, and provoke them to, spiritual wickednesses, pride, envy, malice, etc. These enemies are said to be *in high places,* or in heavenly places, so the word is, taking heaven (as one says) for the whole *expansum,* or spreading out of the air between the earth and the stars, the air being the place from which the devils assault us. Or the meaning may be, *"We wrestle* about heavenly places or heavenly things;" so some of the ancients interpret it. Our enemies strive to prevent our ascent to heaven, to deprive us of heavenly blessings and to obstruct our communion with heaven. They assault us in the things that belong to our souls, and labour to deface the heavenly image in our hearts; and therefore we have

need to be upon our guard against them. We have need of faith in our Christian warfare, because we have spiritual enemies to grapple with, as well as of faith in our Christian work, because we have spiritual strength to fetch in. Thus you see your danger."

Our christian posture is sustained by the power and presence of our Lord and Saviour Jesus Chirst. Our christan stance is vital in business and must be secured and sheilded. I declare that successful discipleship in business, as well as the growth and flourishment of our businesses depends on it.

The apostle Paul gives us pointers on how to stand. He advises us to cover our torso with a breastplate made up of truth and righteousness protecting the vital organs and put peace on our feet. In your hand, hold faith as a shield, "wherewith ye shall be able to quench all the fiery darts of the wicked." Protect your mind by putting the word of God in it, wherein your salvation is found. These are the weapons of our warfare by which we stand.

In Conclusion

GOD'S LAWS ARE DESIGNED TO build a man from within, cultivating him to live in peace of mind, prosperity, good health, and wealth where he is full of virtue and contentment. His wisdom and guidance gives us an advantage in every way. Adherence to the laws of God gives us a right to claim the blessings promised by God. He is our inheritance. All things are ours.

His laws are written in our hearts to be synchronized with every aspect of our lives. Everything we have was a gift from him. We dwell in him, and in him exists our being.

This declaration I give to you, as God gave it to Joshua after the death of Moses. Be it meat for the army of God destined to rein in business. Take from it strength, courage, and the determination of a warrior and win.

Joshua 1:3–8

Every place that the sole of your foot shall tread upon, that have I given unto you, as I said unto Moses. From the wilderness and this Lebanon even unto the great river, the river Euphrates, all the land of the Hittites, and unto the great sea toward the going down of the sun, shall be your coast. There shall not any man be able to stand before thee all the days of thy life: as I was with Moses, so I will be with thee: I will not fail thee, nor forsake thee. Be strong and of a good courage: for unto this people shalt thou divide for an inheritance the land, which I sware unto their fathers to give them. Only be thou strong and very courageous, that thou mayest observe to do according to all the law, which Moses my servant commanded thee: turn not from it to the right hand or to the left, that thou mayest prosper whithersoever thou goest. This book of the law shall not depart out of thy mouth; but thou shalt meditate therein day and night, that thou mayest observe to do according to all that is written therein: for then thou shalt make thy way prosperous, and then thou shalt have good success.

Bibliography

Henry, Matthew. "Complete Commentary on James 3." http://www.searchgodsword.org/com/mhc-com/view. cgi?book=jas&chapter=003.

"Matthew Henry Complete Commentary on the Whole Bible." http://www.biblestudytools.com/commentaries/matthew-henry-complete.

Matthew Henry Commentary, copyright 1991 by Hendrickson Publishers, Inc.

The King James Study Bible (previously published as The Liberty Annotated Study Bible and the Annotated Study Bible, King James Version). Liberty University: 1988.